The Rescue Manual for Parents

by
Ron Luce

4th Printing

The Rescue Manual for Parents
ISBN 1-57778-011-6
Copyright © 1997 by Ron Luce
P. O. Box 2000
Garden Valley, Texas 75771-2000

Dedication

This book is dedicated to parents of teenagers who are desperately trying their best to raise virtuous children, and to all the teenagers who are passionately pursuing God's presence in their lives in order to change the world.

Acknowledgments

A big thank you to my wife, Katie. Together we formulated the principles you are about to read. I also want to express my appreciation to Joni Jones, who edited this book; and the young ladies in my office: Alece Ronzino, Kimberly Houle, Beth McNinch, Charlene Garrett, Sarah Baltzley, Mica Marley, and Dawn Stauffer, who worked many hours typing it. I also want to express appreciation to my executive assistant, Michelle Franzen, for all she has put up with in the process of putting it together. Our prayer is that this book will help parents help their teens — and ultimately help a generation.

Contents

Introduction

Raising teenagers today is not the same as it used to be in generations past. Growing up as a teenager today is not the same as was even 20 years ago. Our society has changed, pressures have changed, temptations have changed, peer pressure has changed — and it has all affected our families. We have so many young people struggling to figure out who they are and who they are supposed to be, and their parents are struggling to figure out how to handle new and different challenges with their young people.

Traveling over the years and speaking to hundreds of thousands of teenagers, I have spent countless hours listening to them share about their families, their struggles, and their challenges. After hearing how parents deal with those challenges, I have prepared this book to offer insight regarding the problems that most commonly face your young person. It is specifically designed to help you break through a number of problem and crisis areas.

You can read through the whole book, or you can use it as a reference manual when you face those crises. If you were to read through the whole thing, you would probably prevent a lot of problem situations before they happen. This book is a "how-to" guide, helping you as a parent get through the difficult situations your parents probably never faced when you were a teenager. It gives you suggestions of things to do, and also discusses the principles behind those things and how to communicate them to your young person.

You will read comments from young people about how they wish their parents would handle the struggles they face. Statistics and comments from experts in the field will provide insight as to why certain problems target certain kids. But most importantly, you will be given a biblical understanding of how to approach various issues.

If you as a parent were to come to me, look me in the eye, and tell me about your young person being in the middle of these situations, what you are about to read is exactly what I would say to you. Since it is impossible to meet one-on-one with the parents of the hundreds of thousands of teens I meet every year, I believe the spiritual principles in this book will help you get through the crises you face. Picture yourself coming into my office to talk about your particular teen's situations or me coming to your home as you read this book to find specific answers to the challenges you are facing. God bless you in your relationship with your teenager!

1

What to do if there is a wall between you and your teen

It happens more often than we would like to admit. In the flurry of life, you have been about your business and your children have been about their business — going to school, being involved in activities, developing relationships. All of a sudden you look across the dinner table and realize you don't really know that young person whom you call your son or daughter. You know their name. You know some of their habits. You know their idiosyncrasies. But you do not know what is going on in their heart, nor in their mind. You don't know the challenges and struggles they are facing.

So you try to start a conversation by asking them what is going on in their life at school and with their friends. Their reaction is, "What do you want to know my business for? Why are you so nosy?" You realize there is not just a gap, but a *wall* keeping you from getting into your teen's world. The sad thing is most parents do not discover the wall in that way. Most times parents discover there is a wall when their teenage son or daughter does something that is almost unthinkable for a parent. It's not until their teen gets pregnant, gets someone else pregnant, gets caught with drugs at a party, or gets arrested that they realize their young person is in a whole other world that they have no idea about.

Following are some quotes from young people giving their perspectives on communication with their parents:

"I feel like there is a wall between me and my parents. They just don't understand how I feel. We have talked about it, and we get along a little better, but things just aren't the way I wish they would be."

"I wish they just would have said they will love and accept me no matter what I choose to do or what friends I have."

"My mom has always chosen what her boyfriends wanted over what her kids needed. I have been sent to family member after family member to take part in raising me. I just wish she would once in a while stop telling me how much of a nuisance I am and pat me on the back."

As you can see, situations like this not only cause a lot of hurt, but build a huge wall. According to Jay Kesler, the top ten mistakes parents make with their children are:

1. Do as I say, not as I do.

2. I'm the adult. I'm right.

3. Because I said so, that's why.

4. You want to be what?

5. This room's a pigsty.

6. Can't you do anything right?

7. Where did you find them?

8. You did what?

9. Do you mind if we talk about something else?

10. I'm kind of busy right now. Could you come back later?[1]

As a result, a wall has been erected between thousands of parents and their teenagers — and most parents are oblivious to it.

When they have finally discovered there is a wall and an entirely different life on the other side, parents find it seemingly impossible to break through. Once we discover there is a problem and a barrier in our communication, we want to fix it right away. "C'mon, let's stop having a wall there and let's just get to know each other." But that is not so easily and quickly done by a young person. They have taken years to build that wall out of brick and stone and do not want to tear it down quickly.

Here are a few principles you can use to break through some of the stony, cold relationships you might have:

1. Most walls begin to go up when someone is hurt. Something has been said or done, either one time or on a number of occasions, that has caused hurt, and no effort has been made to deal with that hurt. As a result, that hurt turns to anger which basically says, "Forget it then. I'm not going to say anything. I'm going to live my own life, do my own thing, and live in my own world." It is impossible to live in this world without getting hurt by someone. Relationships are made out of two or more emotionally complex individuals. The goal is not to avoid the hurt, but to know how to deal with an offense when there is one. Think back through situations you may have been involved in with your young person that may have caused some sort of hurt or turmoil.

It may be divorce, words exchanged in the heat of an argument, something done to them, something repeatedly said to them, or anything that may have caused hurt. Is this to say that it is all your fault? Of course not, but as parents we must take responsibility to find these barriers and tear them down. One teen said:

"I wish that my parents would admit that sometimes they are at fault too."

Once you've identified those areas of possible hurt, go to your young person and ask them to forgive you for specific things you said or did that may have caused any kind of hurt. Don't make a blanket statement and say, "For anything I may have done..." because that sounds wimpy and insincere. Make sure you back up your apology by changing your vernacular or your actions in a certain area to show them you meant it. As you begin to ask for forgiveness, their heart will begin to soften a little bit.

2. Really listen to your kids. James 1:19 says, **Be quick to listen, slow to speak and slow to become angry.** Most of us are slow to listen, quick to speak, and quick to get angry. If you want to really find out what is going on in your teen, begin to really listen to them. As some teenagers put it:

"They should have tried to listen. I don't even try anymore."

"They sent me to counseling without trying to help me themselves. They just gave up on me."

"They wouldn't listen, they overreacted."

CHAPTER ONE . . . **WHAT TO DO IF THERE IS A WALL BETWEEN YOU AND YOUR TEEN**

"When I try to explain my feelings to my mom, she does not understand or see it the same; so she gets upset and snaps at me and tells me I'm wrong. She doesn't listen to my whole story."

"My parents would be the greatest parents in the world if they didn't ask me to be honest about my feelings and then get totally upset if I express my true feelings."

"I wish that my parents would stop talking and listen to what I have to say. I want to tell them so much, but they never stop to listen to me."

Make a habit of listening — not just when you ask, "What's going on in your life?" but when they are sharing stories from school or other things that may seem unimportant to you. Repeat in your mind what they say to you to keep your mind from wandering. Tune in to the feelings behind the words. **The words of a man's mouth are deep waters** (Proverbs 18:4). Behind the words there is a person. They are trying to express something really deep if you'll only listen to them.

Something happens when you listen. The person you're listening to feels like you care enough about them to really tune in. You don't even have to say you care — they can tell you do because you listen to them — and that will make your teen more inclined to listen to you. There is an unspoken reciprocity that makes a person feel obligated to listen to you after you have taken the time to listen to them. Don't make your teen feel obligated. Don't tell them they should listen. Wait for them to *want* to and you'll begin to see the walls break down.

Another teen said:

> "I made a mistake with a boy and they drilled it out of me. Then they told me they were going to talk to him and his parents. That made me feel like I could never trust them with anything again."

As you are listening, be careful how you react to what you hear. Your reaction will determine whether your teen can trust you in the future.

John 15:15 says, **I no longer call you servants, because a servant does not know his master's business. Instead, I have called you friends, for everything that I learned from my Father I have made known to you.** Jesus is redefining His relationship with His disciples, moving them from servants to friends. He shared with them everything His Father shared with Him. He basically told them, "You're not just acquaintances. You're not just people that hang around Me. I have shared My heart with you. You know what goes on inside Me. You know what makes Me tick. Things that My Father whispered to Me I whispered to you. Now you're qualified to be called My friends."

Do you think you should be best friends with your kids? Is it possible to be that kind of friend with your own offspring? One teenager, Stephen Lake from New Cumberland, Pennsylvania, says,

> "My dad is my best friend. We do a lot of things together...He's human and fun to be around. He can be strict. But he's fair. And I respect him for that. I feel free to tell him my concerns. And I trust him."

FAMILY RELATIONSHIPS

Meanwhile, his father, Richard Lake, says,

> "We are good friends...There's a line between being the friend and being the father. I have to use tough love and say no when I think something isn't good for him. And the friendship should be strong enough to be able to say no."

There comes a time in your relationship with your young person when you have to take it from "you're just my son or daughter," to a level of friendship. You begin to do that when you talk to them. Really share your heart. Don't just tell them the rules and regulations and things they need to do. Jesus told the disciples they were qualified to be friends because they knew His heart. If you want to develop a close relationship with your young person, they need to get to know you. A parent might say, "Yeah, well, they don't need to know my business." They don't want to know your *business.* They want to know *you.*

Most young people feel lonely because they don't know their own parents. They sleep under the same roof with strangers every night. The walls in your relationship have been up long enough. It's time to break them down and get to know each other once again. By admitting your failures, asking forgiveness, really listening, and sharing your heart when you talk, you'll be amazed at how much restoration will happen in your relationship with your young person.

2

What to do if your teenager has a rebellious attitude

It's finally here! That cuddly, little infant you anxiously awaited for nine long months has arrived. You're excited about the new addition to your family. You feed your baby, clothe your baby, and change your baby's diapers. You take care of your baby's every need. As your little one grows up you answer all their questions, teach them about life, help them with their spelling homework, and take them to dance lessons, football practice, and after-school activities.

Then all of a sudden, something happens. At about 12 or 13 years of age, it's as though a timer has gone off that has told your child they need to make their own decisions. This little child you cuddled in your arms for years now thinks they have the right and the wisdom to make their own decisions. With their shoulders back and head held high, they inhale and say, "After all, I have lived 13 long years on this earth. I ought to make my own decisions."

Most parents respond with something like, "As long as you are in my house, you are going to do it my way!" It becomes a perpetual argument in the home as to who gets their way. Parents feel they are doomed to fight the battle of teenage rebellion for the next five to six years. "Why are they so rebellious? Why do they fight me on every little thing?"

What is a parent to do? This is what some teenagers have to say about their rebellion:

> "I have a rebellious attitude and every time my parents tell me I do, it makes me even more rebellious."

> "My parents say I am rebellious, but I don't think I am half as bad as I could be. Personally, I think that if they only took a look at their previous life, they would realize how much worse mine could be."

> "Understand why I'm rebellious or selfish and help me to change in a way that won't make me want to rebel more."

> "About three years ago I got into some trouble with the police. I knew my parents were gonna trip out about it — but they got a little violent. It did make me want to never do it again, but it made me fear my parents instead of feeling like I could go and talk to them about stuff. They told me I really didn't want to repent and go to church, but I did. They just assumed they knew my heart, but they didn't. When they assume things it makes me madder."

In dealing with rebellion, we first need to ask ourselves a couple of questions. First, how frequent and intense is the rebellion? According to Kathleen McCoy, Ph.D., "Normal rebellion is sporadic. There are moments of sweetness, calm, and cooperation between outbursts. If on the other hand, rebellion is constant and intense, this can be a sign of underlying emotional problems."[1] Second, is this behavior change drastic for my teenager? Normal rebellious behavior develops over time; but if it is a drastic thing where their behavior

CHAPTER TWO . . . **WHAT TO DO IF YOUR TEENAGER HAS
A REBELLIOUS ATTITUDE**

is completely reverse of what it was, that may be a sign of a deeper problem.

Why do teenagers have such a propensity for rebellion? Dr. James Dobson attributes it to two main reasons. One is hormonal in origin. Because of all the hormonal changes, both males and females may get easily set off. The other is social in nature. Their peer group has become far more important to them than anything else, and the pressures bombarding them to be their own person and identify with a generation have been much more intense than ever before in their lives.[2]

In Josh McDowell's book, *Handbook on Counseling Youth*, the author gives several causes for rebellion: poor relationship with parents, no effort to communicate, a need for control, a lack of boundaries and expectations, an expression of anger and aggression, and the absence of an honest, vulnerable model.[3]

Obviously, there are different stages of rebellion. Some are just minor things like, "I want my own way!" Some teens have an emotionless attitude of resistance and a hardened heart that says, "I don't care what you say or do, I'm going to do my own thing!"

Let's look at a few principles that will help you understand where your young person is coming from. One of the most important is that rules without relationship equals rebellion. As one young lady said, "One of the worst things my parents have done is give me a 'no' answer, without explaining why."

Most parents think the rightful responsibility of a parent is to provide food and a roof over their teen's head without developing much of a relationship with them. As a result, your young person might as well be living in a boarding school — just a place to live with a bunch of rules. When asked about a rule, most parents never explain the reason for it. "Because I say so, that is why!" Many times parents don't even know why they have that rule. Their parents had that rule, and if it was good enough for them, it's good enough for their kids.

I can remember when my mom told me that people shouldn't have sex outside of marriage. I was probably 13 or 14 years old and I had never heard that before. I had never heard it was wrong. I asked, "Why is it wrong?" She replied, "Just because it is." In an innocent, not condemning way, I said, "Well, you did." She said, "Well, that was different."

Kids want to know the *why* of the rules and understand the reasons behind them. That is why it is important to understand the principles in this book. But in addition to that, your young person needs to know the person who is implementing the rules.

Many companies are run better than some families. Even companies have reasons for their rules. A wisely run company has relationships between managers and subordinates that are more than just "Do what I say!" A wise manager cares about the personal lives of the people they supervise. Let it not be said that a company down the street cares more about their employees and knows more about what is going on in their lives than we know about our own teenagers!

When your teen feels forced to obey a rule but feels that you do not know them or care about them, it produces a rebellious attitude that says, "You don't care about me, so I don't care about your stupid rules. I'm going to do what I want to do!"

CHAPTER TWO . . . **WHAT TO DO IF YOUR TEENAGER HAS A REBELLIOUS ATTITUDE**

One of the biggest goals as a parent is to have a final product of young adults who are responsible, productive members of society, church, and the kingdom of God. It's never been our dream for our kids to be sitting on our couch, eating chips, and watching television when they are 35 years old. We want them to be responsible, and they begin to get the itch for responsibility when they are teenagers. They want to have some of their own "say-so" regarding their lives.

Your young person wants to be able to make some of their own decisions. They don't want to be dictated to anymore. Even though you may still see them as young and not knowing what to do or where to go, they see themselves as quite skilled in life and wanting to have some control of their destiny.

Some parents are like an iron fist, "As long as you're in my house, I am going to make the decisions. Just do it this way!" This approach doesn't give their young person a chance to make any decisions or learn responsibility. Other parents go to the other extreme, and say, "Well, I can't really do anything about it anyway, so I let them do what they want to do." Neither approach is very wise.

Your young person's need for responsibility is the need to be able to say, "I made this decision and I realize it was a good decision." If you make all the decisions while your child lives under your roof, they will never understand and learn how to make decisions on their own.

If you tell them not to drink simply because "I say so" and force them not to do it, they'll go on a drinking binge when they go to college. You'll wonder, "Why? What did I do? They never drank when they were under my roof." Maybe you didn't teach them how to make the best decisions while they were under your roof, so when they were faced with making the decision on their own, they didn't know how to deal with all the pressures.

A teen's desire to be given responsibility may be perceived as rebellion. But just because your young person wants to make their own decisions in life doesn't mean they are rebellious — it means they are starting to grow up! Give them some opportunities to make decisions about what they do with their free time. It doesn't mean you let them make decisions about everything. Start out with small decisions, such as spending the night at a friend's house even though they need to study for a test. You know they have a test, they say they've already studied, but your inclination would be to make them stay home and study more. Give them the opportunity to decide what is best.

Once they show themselves faithful in these small opportunities by making good decisions, you can allow them to make bigger decisions. The goal is getting them to make all their own decisions before they ever leave the house. I know parents who have said they don't have any rules for their 14-year-old children because they make all the right decisions on their own. "I tell them they can stay out as late as they want. And they always come in at 10:00 because they have learned to be responsible while they were young."

Children need rules. Adults need responsibility. Adolescents need advice. We know we have to set very strong and clear rules for children or they will not have any structure in their lives. We just discussed the adult's need for responsibility that they start thirsting for when they are young. Think about the first job you ever had. You were so excited to be making your

CHAPTER TWO . . . **WHAT TO DO IF YOUR TEENAGER HAS A REBELLIOUS ATTITUDE**

own money. You were thrilled over the responsibility that was yours. That yearning for taking responsibility for your own life started when you were a teenager. What do teenagers need? They don't need just a bunch of rules, nor do they need all the responsibility to decide everything about their lives. Meet somewhere in the middle by giving them wise advice.

Take the situation about the teen who wants to spend the night at a friend's house, but has a test the next day. You tell them, "This is my advice. I think you need to stay home and study for your test. But I'm not going to tell you what to do. I will let you make your own decision on this." So you let them make their own decision. If they made a great decision, either to stay home or to spend the night, and got an A on the test, you can let your chest swell. "You're a chip off the old block. I knew you would make the right decision." If they made a bad decision, it is important how you respond. Do not slam them, put them down, or make them feel like a nothing. You're the one who gave them the chance to make the decision.

Your young person will make some bad decisions. They're a teenager. They're a young person. One of our biggest tasks is to teach our young people how to make wise decisions. We do that by giving them advice. Say you gave your teen advice but they didn't take it. They went and spent the night and got an F on the test. Talk through that decision with them. "Let's talk about it. What made you want to go even though I advised you not to?" Listen to what they tell you. Then ask, "If you were in the same situation again, would you do the same thing? Why or why not? Look at all the people who got F's all the way through high school. Where are they today? Is that the kind of person you want to be?" The next time they get a chance to make a decision, give them advice and let them choose for themselves again.

There are going to be some decisions that you might let them make too early. The big question is, what decisions do you make for your young person and what decisions do you let them make? That is between you and God. Pray and find out from the Lord. Sometimes you'll say, "I'll let them make this decision," and you realize that maybe you shouldn't have. They are too young or not mature enough. Some young people are ready for certain decisions earlier than others. There is not a magical date and time to use as a deciding factor.

The next time that decision opportunity arises, you can say, "I'll make it for you this time. I was wrong and shouldn't have let you make it the first time." By the time they are 18, your young person should be weaned from having all their decisions made for them. They should be able to make almost all the decisions about their life in a mature, responsible way.

It is much better for them to make bad decisions under your protective umbrella, where you can go back and talk about the failure and how to do it right the next time, than for them to leave your house and make all the wrong decisions. Once out from your protective covering, they don't always seek your advice or care what you have to say about it. Instead of propping them up all the time to keep them from falling, allow them to make a few bad decisions. Then go back and talk through those issues so they can make better decisions for the rest of their life.

3

What to do if your teen lies, or you suspect they lie, regularly

It begins with a question. Does your young person really mean what they say? Do they realize you know the real truth about a particular situation? You shake it off, deciding they couldn't remember what really happened. But then you find a few more inconsistencies in their story about what they were doing that night when you thought they were somewhere else. Later you find something in their room they say they are not involved with and have never even tried. At this point, your suspicions are raised. Every time you ask them about something you suspect is different from what they are telling you, they always have ample explanation. You have either caught them red-handed in a bald-faced lie, or there are so many inconsistencies, you have no logical conclusion other than to think they are definitely lying to you.

As some teens put it:

"I find myself lying to my parents. I wish that lying wasn't the only way we could keep things cool between us."

"I wish my parents would say that being honest and getting in trouble is more important than lying and not getting in trouble. I have no reason to tell the truth because even when I do, they don't praise me for my honesty."

"I lie because they don't trust me and I need to be with my friends — so I need to lie."

"I wish they wouldn't blow up at me so easily when I do something bad or wrong, so I wouldn't have to lie about it."

"I wish they wouldn't have overreacted to things I have told them in the past so that I'd have the freedom now to tell them the whole truth."

I don't want to lay the whole burden of teens' lying on the parents, but from the teens' perspective, the more we respond irrationally, the more it pushes them to continue to lie.

Recent studies have found that 91 percent of parents lie routinely and 59 percent lie regularly to their kids.[1] If this is the example we are setting for our young people, it shouldn't surprise us that they are lying to us. Some people resolve that teens are just going to lie — it's part of life and you can't do anything about it. Forty-five percent of born-again teens believe lying is sometimes necessary, compared to 71 percent of teens not born again.[2]

In addition, teenagers' perspectives on truth vary. When asked if what is right for one person in a given situation might not be right for another person in a similar situation, 92 percent of born-again teens agreed and 90 percent of teens not born again agreed. When given the statement, "When it comes to matters of morals and ethics, truth means different things to different people. No one can be absolutely positive that they know the truth," 66 percent of born-again teens agreed, and 87 percent of those not born-again agreed. When told, "There is no such thing as absolute truth — two people could define truth in conflicting ways and both could still be correct," 59 percent of born-again teenagers said they agreed while 78 percent of teenagers not born-again agreed.[3] We have a lot of people who say they are born-again who still do not have a clear picture of what truth is all about. No wonder it is so easy to lie!

If lying is an issue or is becoming an issue in your home, you have a bigger problem than you think. Parents tend to think that at least lying is not as bad as getting pregnant or getting drunk. But in reality, you know a good liar can cover all that up. Perpetual lies are like cancer in a relationship. The very essence of a lie is "I can't trust you with the truth, so I will tell you what I think you want to hear." If that is the case, the very core of your relationship is a fallacy. There is no relationship. Your blood may be in their veins, but there is no relationship.

If your young person has to lie to you about the small things and finds they can get away with it, why would they not lie to you about the big things? Pretty soon, they are living a whole other life and their identity is totally shrouded from you in a cleverly manufactured set of lies. Who I was in school and who I was in front of my parents were two completely different persons. My parents had no idea of my personality, my attitudes, or my actions at school. I was meticulous at weaving together a tapestry of deceit so they would never know what I was really like at school.

If lying is the problem, you have no basis for a relationship. The very foundation of a relationship — trust and respect — is null and void. There is no basis for trust, and it takes *trust* to develop a relationship. I say this to alert you. If you suspect lying, don't blow it off as not being that big of a sin. Go after it and get to the bottom of it before it develops into something much more serious.

Teach your children from an early age the importance of truth, the nature of a lie, and what integrity is all about. Don't assume that your young person knows it is wrong to lie, but help them to understand why. I recently taught my daughters about integrity as they were playing a game of *Twister*. We discussed that if one of their elbows accidentally hits the ground and they lifted it back up before anyone saw, they are not really being honest. They are still young, but teaching them to be truthful in their *heart* at a very young age will permeate every area of their lives.

One day, one of our interns was sitting next to one of my little girls while eating lunch at the Teen Mania cafeteria. My daughter said, "Here, do you want these cookies? I'm not supposed to have them." No one was there to stop her. She could have eaten them secretly, but she chose to do what was right.

Here are a few tips for imparting principles regarding truth to your young person:

First, ask yourself, "How much do I lie?" Our society is so bombarded with lies that you may be telling an untruth and not even realize it. You may be exaggerating the truth, stretching the truth, or telling a "white lie." Have you ever had your spouse answer the phone for you and you say, "If it is so-and-so, tell them I'm not here"? Boom! You've just lied! You are telling your kids, "Do what I say, don't do what I do." You have just sent a message to them loud and clear that it is okay to lie when it is convenient or when there is something we don't want someone else to know. Assess your own truthfulness to see what kind of example you are setting.

Jesus said Satan is the "father of lies." (See John 8:44.) Teach your young person that lying is a character flaw. It is the very essence of the devil. He lies to us to trick us and pull us away from God. He manipulates, he deceives, and he tricks — not always with a blatant lie but with shadows and shades of the truth. The best lie in the world is the one that stays as close to the truth as possible with only a little bit of error. But that small bit of error constitutes a lie.

Lying is the very nature of Satan himself. He lies to people about God. He tells them that God is no good — that God wants to hurt them and mess up their lives. He plants lies in the hearts and minds of spouses, making them think the other one is cheating on them. He plants lies in the hearts of kids to make them think their parents don't care about them or love them. He is a liar. He is the chief of liars, and the king of liars. He's the best liar there ever was.

When we participate in lies it does something to our character. We become more and more like the devil. That is the harsh reality, but it is the truth.

Teach your teen about the nature of truth. James 5:12 says, **Let your "Yes" be yes, and your "No," no.** Let your word count for something. When you say, "Yes, I'm going to do something," you shouldn't have to swear by this or that. Saying you will do something should be enough for someone to trust your word. Teach your young person the value of truth and of truthfulness.

Teach them about integrity. Proverbs 11:3 says, **The integrity of the upright guides them.** That means, if you are full of integrity and truthfulness, you are not always trying to keep up with which lie you told to whom or wondering if you are going to be caught. If you walk with integrity, you walk securely. You are safe. Nothing is going to be found out about you because everything is already known. You don't have to walk on eggshells and try to recreate the same lies you had before. You can walk securely and confidently.

Ask yourself why your teen feels the need to lie to you. What is it they are trying to hide? Why are there secret parts of their life they don't want you to know about? Are they ashamed of them? Afraid of what you will say? Afraid of what you will do? If they are lying about some small things, maybe there are large areas of greater concern they are also lying about.

What has caused such a gap and a barrier in your relationship that they feel the need to have a secret life? This issue is more important than the actual lying itself and gets back to the actual heart of the relationship. If the relationship is laced with lies, there is really no relationship. It is one or two fake people pretending they are interacting in an honest way.

Instill in your young person an understanding of this principle, and mean it when you say, "Whatever you do, don't ever lie to me." Your young person needs to know that whatever has transpired, you are the first person they come running to. Carry

CHAPTER THREE . . . **WHAT TO DO IF YOUR TEEN LIES, OR YOU SUSPECT THEY LIE, REGULARLY**

yourself in a way that says "No matter what you have done, no matter how bad it is, it is worse to lie."

Your teen needs to feel a freedom to come to you in every situation. It doesn't mean they are granted immunity over any bad thing they do if they just tell you the truth about it. It means that the consequences of lying about it are so much more severe that it makes them not want to lie. They also learn the value of coming clean. This will help them in their relationship with God. So many times people do things they know God doesn't want them to do, and just like Adam they try to hide, sneak around, and pretend they didn't do anything. The first step towards getting whole is for your young person to admit that they really blew it — they made a mistake.

Teach them the value of truthfulness so they will not try to live a secret life. Find ways of rewarding them and blessing them for telling the truth in small matters and in big matters. You want to know that when you look your young person in the eyes and they tell you something, you can trust them — you can believe them, and if you need to, you can go to bat for them and stand up for them based on the word they gave you, knowing it is the truth.

Building this kind of open, truthful environment into your home and your relationship puts you on the road towards a great, wholesome relationship with your young person. There will always be bumps along the way, but at least you know there is a legitimate relationship, because there is honesty between you.

If you suspect your young person is lying, don't constantly accuse them of lying. If you have caught them in an occasional lie, don't assume *everything* is a lie. You might question it in your mind, but don't always vocalize it. If they have committed to tell you the truth, then grant them that trust. Make them prove to you that they really are telling you the truth.

Don't always point your finger and accuse them of lying. In fact, you don't even want to say the "L" word. If you think your teen is lying and sneaking around, what you need to do is get enough facts to back up what you really think. Then still don't say the "L" word, but sit your young person down when you have enough facts. Say something like this, "Johnny, remember how I've taught you the value of telling the truth? Remember how I've told you Satan is the father of lies? Remember how I've told you that no matter what you've done, you can come to me and tell me the truth? Now if you were to be completely truthful about this situation, is there anything else you would want to tell me?"

Instead of accusing them of lying, give them a chance to come clean and to empty their heart. It is good for their soul and for their heart. It is better for forgiveness and for your relationship. If they respond by saying, "No," say, "Now, Johnny, think about sitting right in front of the throne of God and having God ask you — is there anything else? It doesn't matter what the consequences are or even what you've done. At this moment, what matters is that you are being truthful about this. Is there anything else you want to say?" Then wait in silence for their response.

CHAPTER THREE . . . **WHAT TO DO IF YOUR TEEN LIES, OR YOU SUSPECT THEY LIE, REGULARLY**

You then have a choice. You can say, "Okay, I trust you and believe you," if you don't have any *evidence* to the opposite. If you do, you might show them a little bit of that evidence, but not all of it and say, "Johnny, so-and-so told me that you were here at this time. And you said you were at this other place. Are you sure you are being completely truthful? Is there anything else you can remember at all?"

What you're doing is showing them you know a little bit more than they thought you knew. So now they don't know how much you do know. That might provoke them to be honest. If not, show a little bit more of the cards in your hand. Tell them a little more of what you know and give them the chance to be truthful. You don't want to ever come out and say, "You lied about this and this."

Keep giving them chances to come clean. If they still refuse all the way through the process, show them your complete hand. Hopefully, at that point they will break and say, "I'm sorry I lied to you." Once they have confessed, don't get mad and say, "Well, you stupid kid! What did you lie to me for?" Talk about it.

"Why did you feel like you had to lie to me?" Give them some consequences for lying, but more importantly, talk through it. Don't just talk about the thing they did, but talk about the lying issue as well. Let them know they compounded the issue by lying about the whole situation.

You need to have a trustworthy relationship, one where you can count on the fact that your young person always tells you the truth. Make a big point about the lying issue, teaching them the importance of truthfulness, integrity, and being completely above board.

Young people do not learn about truthfulness and integrity by talking about it one time. Start when they are young — or now, wherever they are at — and begin to share from the Scriptures the importance and value of living a life of total integrity without any lies. As you begin to plant seeds and principles into their heart, they are going to begin to value telling the truth on their own. They will do it not because Mom and Dad told them to or because they might get into trouble if they don't, but because they know it is right and they will be blessed for it.

4

What to do if your teen says, "I don't know," every time you try to start a conversation

We all know we should spend time talking to our kids, but many of us do not know where to begin. We feel we are doing our job as a parent by asking them questions about their life, but we get tired of hearing the proverbial "I don't know."

The problem is not that your young person does not know. The problem is not that you did not ask the right question. The problem is the lack of a wholesome relationship. Many parents go for the jugular vein right away in trying to figure out what is going on with their young people. We ask the "Big Kahuna" questions.

What your teen is really saying in their "I don't know" response is that they don't know if they want to tell you, not that they don't know the answer. Of course, young people go through phases where they genuinely do not know how they feel or what they think about certain situations.

Most young people and parents live in two different worlds. Some young people say:

> "I say 'I don't know' every time my parents try to start a conversation with me. They ask me what is wrong and I

don't want to tell them because I don't want to hurt them."

"I wish my parents would say that I can tell them anything and they would listen to me until I am done; that they want to help me tell them what is going on in my life and that they want to be close to me."

One teen's explanation for the "I don't know" problem:

"Sometimes I don't even feel like I want to discuss stuff because I don't want to get in a fight. Sometimes it's just better not to bring it up."

In a recent study, a group of teenagers identified several points they regard as important when their parents talk with them.

1. Tell us you love us even if we act like we don't want to hear it.

2. If we have a major problem, help us solve it. Don't solve it for us. If you do, we'll never learn how to function as adults.

3. Never stop talking to us. You're the only ones we can count on for reassurance and love.[1]

A few tips for getting through this area:

1. Before you go for the jugular, talk about peripheral issues. Talk about other things they are interested in, such as sports, movies, or music. Develop a relationship rather than demanding them to tell you the answer to some big important question. Your young person will do anything to

protect their emotions and feelings from being slammed. They are normal human beings who want to know that someone cares about *them* — not just their problems or one area of their life. Have great patience in developing a warm enough relationship so that when you ask a question, you will be less likely to hear, "I don't know."

2. Listen to conversations they bring up. Listen to what they talk about and use that to lead you into a deeper conversation with them. If they are talking about a certain event that just happened, don't change the subject. Ask them simple questions to show you are interested. "How did you feel when they said that to you?" "What were you thinking when such and such happened to you?" Asking questions will show them you care about what they have to say. By asking heart-oriented questions about whatever they are talking about — whether it is friends, music, school, or a new movie — you will work your way into their heart. Always have your ear tuned in to statements that come from their heart. Look for every conversation to tell you something about their heart and what is going on in their mind — not because you are a giant probe, but because you constantly have your radar sensors looking for information that reveals what makes them tick and how they are really feeling. When they sense you care about them in that way, you are going to hear the response "I don't know" less and less.

One young person said:

"If I would say anything other than, 'I don't know,' it would turn into a big argument with my mom. I wish she would just understand me and not bother me."

Be careful how you respond to both the good and bad news your teen brings to you. Have they ever experienced a great victory at school or on their team, and as they excitedly tell you, you say, "Oh that's great," as you continue to read the paper? Or have they brought home some really heartbreaking news that may not sound very upsetting to you, but may have been devastating for them? Do not patronize them with, "Oh, that's too bad." Sometimes parents blow up when they hear bad news — they get angry, cuss, lose their temper, and scream. Deciding to control your attitude and your words toward your young person is a big step in getting through the "I don't knows."

Remember, they are really saying, "I don't know how you are going to respond. I don't know if I want to *see* how you are going to respond." You ask them a question and they tell you, "I don't know," because they are tired of either getting no response or one that barks down their throat. Take a deep breath and control your heart, mind, and emotions on a daily basis with your young person. They'll be able to see that you are not set off by a little spark and they don't have to walk on eggshells around you. As a result, when you ask the important questions, they'll be more likely to be straightforward and honest.

3. If your teen answers a question with, "I don't know," ask them, "What would you say if you did know?" It causes them to rethink the issue. The fact is they do know. Sometimes they are simply not in touch with how they feel or what they think. You would be amazed at how often they will actually come back with a response if you use a simple little conversation starter.

5

What to do if your teenager does not enjoy being at home or goes out every spare minute

Are you starting to get a complex? Does it seem like every time you think you are going to have a little time to spend with your teenager they have something more important to do? It's one thing when it is a sports activity or something school-associated, but it's another thing when it seems like your young person just doesn't want to be at home.

They find every excuse to be with a friend or to do this or that, and you think, *I brought them into this world. I have taken care of them all these years and all of a sudden they don't want to be with me.* They might say things like, "You are boring. This house is boring and I just don't want to be here." Some young people have said:

"I am gone a lot because my mom always has something to do. I wish she'd actually try to make time for me, then I might stay home more often."

"Whenever I am at home, I feel like I am walking on eggshells. I feel like no matter what I say, I am going to start an argument."

"I wish my dad would stay home more often. He leaves at 4:45 A.M. and gets home about 7:00 P.M. I get so bored at home and this is why I am always gone."

"If my parents would back off more and let me stay closed up in my room by myself, I would stay home more often."

"I wish my parents would ask me to do more things as a family instead of staying home alone all of the time."

What is a parent to do?

First of all, understand you are not alone. This is a normal part of growing up. Psychologists have identified that in the first phase of life, a child's primary relationships are with parents. Children care about what their parents think and what they do. Their whole life revolves around interaction with their parents. Then there comes a point during adolescence when the primary relationship shifts from parents to friends as they learn to interact socially. This is healthy, because for the rest of your teen's life you want them to know how to interact socially in a healthy way. So don't feel left behind just because they want to be with friends. It doesn't mean you cannot influence what friends they have (see chapter 20) or the amount of time they spend with them. Their decision to spend time with friends doesn't mean you are a bad parent or that there is something inherently wrong or bad about you. They are simply growing up.

How busy have you been throughout the life span of your young person — even when they were little children? Were you busy, busy, busy with work and activities? Maybe now things

CHAPTER FIVE . . . **WHAT TO DO IF YOUR TEENAGER DOES NOT ENJOY BEING AT HOME OR GOES OUT EVERY SPARE MINUTE**

have slowed down for you, so you expect your young person to drop everything to be with you. Maybe they have learned to develop a life totally independent from you. Most parents do not understand that. They think, *now I am here. Why don't they want to be with me now that I am making time for them?*

There could be some hurt and resentment in their heart because of the time you did not spend with them when they were younger. You weren't there for them when they needed you, so they have learned how to get along without you. If this is the case, it will take some time to rebuild that relationship and show them you are truly sorry. It will take a while for them to realize you want to spend time getting to know them.

Your home needs to be like a greenhouse for your young person. Make it a place where they really want to spend time. That doesn't necessarily mean having a television for them to watch whenever they want to. It has to do more with how your home looks and feels, and the attitudes displayed around the home. Some young people have every high-tech toy you could imagine but don't want to be at home. They feel like they're always walking on eggshells — someone is going to get mad and blow up at someone else. Who wants to be around that?

You may have to search your own heart and deal with attitudes in your own life. Maybe you need to set up rules and guidelines that are less harsh or more harsh, depending on the situation you find yourself in. Create an atmosphere so that when your teen comes home they feel welcome, like they have arrived in a haven. They are in a place where they know they are safe and protected from the world.

Your teen needs to feel wanted. Let them know you look forward to them being there. They need to feel you care enough about them to cook their favorite food. Do you respect their opinion enough that you take their advice on things, such as painting a room a color they chose? Make your home a refuge from the harsh realities of this world that is trying to tear your teen away from God and beat them up on the inside.

Don't demand that your young person stay home during their free time just for the sake of their being there. You can have them there physically, but if their heart is not there, is it going to do much good? I suggest you include exciting events for them to do in your calendar of social activities.

Make your home the place young people in your community will want to hang out when they come over to see your son or daughter. Don't just say, "Stay home." Instead say, "Hey! Why don't you invite some friends over? You can rent a video, buy some snacks and drinks, and I'll foot the bill."

Plan activities to do as a family and with friends that seem bigger than life — something your young person could not do on their own with their friends, because it costs money or they don't have the resources to do it. You are not trying to buy your young person's love! You are trying to show them you care enough about them to provide something fun for them to do in the context of your own home.

They should feel like their home is not just a place where they eat and sleep. It is a place where they have fun with their family and friends. Make your home a place your young person is not embarrassed or ashamed to invite friends to, but they are excited to invite them. It is going to cost you money and time, but your teen is only young once.

Give them a teenage legacy to look back on. I have talked to young people that said, "My friends love coming over to my house. They call my parents 'Mom' and 'Dad'." Your teen needs to feel important enough that you have really thought through to plan an event — something that is really awesome. It will cost money, but in the end it will be worth it when your young person looks back on the fond memories and times around the house with their friends there — and you were the champion. You helped to shape them in your greenhouse — not to mention keeping them off the streets, away from the wrong parties, and out of compromising situations where trouble could have accidentally sprouted up in their life.

6

What to do if you are a dad who wants to develop a close relationship with your daughter

I see it almost every weekend as I travel to "Acquire the Fire" conventions across North America — young ladies busted, confused, hurt, and brokenhearted because of the shallowness or lack of relationship with their fathers. I see them stream to the altar with makeup smeared all over their faces from the tears they have cried, asking God to be their Father, because their biological father is not there, physically or emotionally.

You don't have to see an altar call like that, though, to see the evidence of the lack of relationship between girls and their dads. You can see it in the eyes of girls wearing heavy makeup, short skirts, and flirting with the guys all the time. You can see their insecurity manifested by how they look before they leave the house.

They can't stand the thought of walking out of the house without bombarding themselves with every ounce of glamour that is sure to jerk the necks of every guy who walks by. They are desperate for male attention. Any male will do. Any kind of attention will do. They want someone to tell them they are pretty. They want someone to tell them they are worthwhile.

In *Parenting Isn't for Cowards*, Dr. James Dobson writes:

"Most psychologists believe, and I am one of them, that all future romantic relationships to occur in a girl's life will be influenced positively or negatively by the way she perceives and interacts with her dad. If he is an alcoholic and a bum, she will spend her life trying to replace him in her heart. If he is warm and nurturing, she will look for a lover to equal him. If he thinks she is beautiful, worthy, and feminine, she will be inclined to see herself that way. But if he rejects her as unattractive and uninteresting, she is likely to carry self-esteem problems into her adult years."[1]

He will turn the hearts of the fathers to their children, and the hearts of the children to their fathers.

Malachi 4:6

Your daughter may or may not be struggling with low self-esteem, but fathers need to make sure they are doing the things that will endear their daughters to them. Here are several ways you can do that:

The first thing to do is pray for your daughter. Ask God to really turn your heart toward her, to help you really love her with a godly, fatherly love, and to help you see her as God sees her. What you do to encourage a relationship should not be just a physical activity done out of obligation. Spending time together and doing things with her are great, but make sure it is a result of your heart genuinely being drawn towards her through prayer.

Continue to pray for her. Think about what she is going through at school and with friends, and pray for those specific areas. Listen to stories and things that are going on in her life, and pray for those things until your heart is overflowing with supernatural love from the Father. It will take more than just one prayer time. It will take more than just a week or two. Take a couple of months to pray specifically for her and for your heart to be endeared toward her.

As a father and as the man of the house, God has called you to be the priest of your home. As a priest, you are to be the spiritual head. Think about it. What have you done to be the spiritual father to your daughter? How have you helped her grow in the Lord? Have you encouraged her in her walk with God?

As you pray for her and let God woo your heart towards her, ask the Lord what to say to her. "Lord, what would You want me to share with her? What scriptures would encourage her? How can she mature in her character and her walk with You?"

She needs to know that not only are you her biological father, but in a very real way you are helping her grow spiritually. She needs to know she can come to you for advice, counsel, and encouragement because she knows you hear the voice of God. She knows you have wisdom because you have read the Scriptures and you understand the wise way of living. That means you need to be filling yourself up by reading the Bible, reading books about being a good father, listening to tapes, and writing down nuggets that you can share later. Constantly pour into your daughter spiritually. She'll enjoy being around you because she'll feel like she is growing. You are blessing her, encouraging her, and helping her to take the next step in the Lord, rather than shoving God down her throat.

Is there anything you have said or done in the past that has hurt her in any way and marred her relationship with you? It's amazing how one comment from a father can totally destroy the relationship a daughter has with her dad and can send the relationship in a totally different direction. Were you an absent father much of her childhood? Have you made comments about her looks or her weight? This is not to throw a guilt trip on you, but to help you realize the things that you need to deal with. Until these things are dealt with, they can keep a distance between you.

Your relationship with your daughter will directly mirror her perception of what the Father God is like. Daughters who have been abused, put down, discouraged, or disillusioned by their physical fathers often reflect that kind of perspective toward their spiritual Father. This is not just good advice to treat your daughters nicely. This could affect where she spends eternity!

If your daughter perceives her Father God as a mean, demanding, resentful, cold Father Who doesn't share His emotions or care enough to really listen to her and be a part of her life, she has no reason to want to be close to Him. Our responsibility is to represent the heart of Father God. If we are successful in representing the kind of Father He truly is, she will have the desire to know her Father in heaven.

Show your daughter the appropriate amount of male affection. Gordon McDonald writes:

"Because a father is the first man to whom a daughter relates, that relationship is incredibly important — more so than most men realize. Daughters need to know that their fathers accept them as women and not just as little girls...Daughters also need physical affection from their fathers. Some fathers feel embarrassed about giving attention to their daughters. They may have to push themselves and deliberately demonstrate affection until it becomes natural."[2]

Most fathers operate on one extreme or the other in the affection department. Some will obviously err in being too affectionate and making their daughters feel uncomfortable. There are some fathers who have taken it to such an extreme that they have actually abused or violated their daughters. Then there are fathers who go to the other extreme and have a strictly platonic, nuts-and-bolts type of relationship. They shake her hand and never physically get close.

There is a balance in the middle where your daughter needs to know the wholesome affection of her father. That is, kissing her on the cheek, hugging her tight around the neck, and putting your arm around her when you're watching a television program together. It should not be a foreign experience for your daughter to feel your arm around her.

James Dobson describes a daughter's need for appropriate affection:

"With girls, physical contact (especially the affectionate type) increases in importance as she becomes older and reaches a zenith at around the age of 11. What a critical time!...A child growing up in a home where parents use eye and physical contact will be comfortable with himself and other people. They will have an easy time communicating with others, and consequently be well-liked and have good self-esteem. Appropriate and frequent eye and physical contact are two of the most precious gifts we can give our children...A father helps his daughter approve of herself by showing her that he approves of her. He does this by...unconditional love, eye contact, and physical contact, as well as focused attention. A daughter's need for her father to do this begins as early as two years of age. This need, although important at younger ages, becomes greater as the girl grows older and approaches that magic age of 13. One problem in our society is that as a girl grows older, a father usually feels increasingly uncomfortable about giving his daughter the affection she needs. This is extremely unfortunate. Yes, fathers, we must ignore our discomfort and give our daughters what is vital to them for their entire lives."[3]

God made us with a mother and a father because He knows it takes affection and emotional contact from both. It is male and female affection, fatherly and motherly affection in our lives, that brings wholesomeness to children. When your daughter doesn't get wholesome affection from her father, she will look for affection somewhere else from another male. The tragedy is, they don't know what they're looking for. They just want someone to make them feel loved.

CHAPTER SIX . . . **WHAT TO DO IF YOU ARE A DAD WHO WANTS TO DEVELOP A CLOSE RELATIONSHIP WITH YOUR DAUGHTER**

If they don't get that kind of affection or approval in a godly, fatherly way from their dads, they are going to look for it in the wrong way. Hence, so many young ladies become promiscuous and advertise their bodies to get attention from males. Some, who feel that no matter what they do they can't get the right kind of affection, get themselves involved in sexual immorality — hoping that just for a moment, someone will give them the kind of affection that will fill their heart — only to find later they still feel empty.

What they are really looking for is wholesome male affection from their dad. If they get plenty of that, they won't need to look for affection from a guy, a date, or an unwholesome romantic relationship. If some guy starts getting sweet on your daughter, giving her all kinds of compliments and accolades on how cute she is, the first thing that should pop in her mind is that her dad tells her that all the time.

Her heart should not be overwhelmed just because some guy spoke sweet words to her. She knows her father gives her wholesome affection and says those kinds of things to her and makes her feel valuable all the time. She won't be starstruck and fall into a trance when a guy pays attention to her because she is used to wholesome godly affection and attention.

In addition, she learns to recognize unwholesome, ungodly affection or attention, and it becomes a disdain, a disgrace, and a put-down to her — not something she longs for. When we treat our daughters with respect, valuing them as precious before God, unashamed to hug them and kiss them on the cheek, to tell them we love them, and to shower them with compliments, we are putting protective measures in their lives.

This keeps them from the wolves out there who are trying to give them unwholesome affection that can ultimately destroy their lives.

7

What to do if you are a dad who wants to develop a close relationship with your son

It has happened hundreds of times during ministry time. Thousands of young people have come forward for prayer regarding their parents. I specifically address teenage guys who have had a tough time with their dad, feel far away from them, or have bitterness or resentment towards their dad. I tell them, "It's time to let go. It's time to forgive." Young men lift their hands all over the arena and begin to sob. When we pray a prayer of forgiveness together, their hearts begin to break as they confront the hurt they have felt for so long towards their dads.

When I pray with them and speak with them individually, I sense the depth of their pain. As I wrap my arms around them and hug them, they latch on to me and begin to sob out of their inner gut. The pain is so deep that no bandage or no doctor could ever heal it. They hold on to me and won't let go. Many of them have been hurting for so long with a pain so deep that they forgot they were hurting. They thought it was normal to have a cold relationship with their dad — an empty, shallow, meaningless relationship. They thought it was par for the course. Every time I hold one of those teenage men in my arms, hugging them with a bear hug, I feel like I am holding teenage America in my arms.

David Blankenhorn, chairman of National Fatherhood Initiative and president of the Institute for American Values, refers to fatherlessness as "the most urgent social problem of our generation." Kids without fathers are more likely to:

Drop out of high school

Get pregnant as a teen

Abuse drugs

Be in trouble with the law

Be a victim to physical or sexual abuse

Face emotional problems[1]

In 1960, 17.5 percent of teens lived apart from their biological fathers. By 1990, that percentage had doubled to 36 percent. By the turn of the century, nearly one-half of American children may be going to sleep each night in a different house than their father's. That's 50 percent of the nation's children!

Out-of-wedlock births are expected to surpass divorce as a cause of fatherlessness, rising to 40 percent by the year 2000. The tripling of teen suicides since the mid-1950s, the rise in chemical abuse, and the decline in SAT scores by 75 points between 1960 and 1990 are all trends that social scientists say were impacted by the absence of fathers.[2]

CHAPTER SEVEN . . . **WHAT TO DO IF YOU ARE A DAD WHO WANTS TO DEVELOP A CLOSE RELATIONSHIP WITH YOUR SON**

What is it about us fathers that makes us have such a tough time getting close to our sons? The expectations our society puts on us to be macho, cool, hip, and not to cry or be emotional takes an amazing toll on our sons. In our "machoism" we have passed on a legacy of cold-hearted relationships and missed the very richness of a heart-to-heart connection with our sons. Let's look at some of the principles regarding our relationship with our sons:

First of all, why is it so hard?

Our society says that a "real" man doesn't cry. A real man doesn't get close to other men. A real man doesn't hug other men. We think all the touchy, feely stuff is only reserved for ladies and their tea parties. We men get together, watch a ball game, grunt a little bit, and have great fellowship. Although it is true that camaraderie is built differently for guys than for girls, there sure are a lot of guys who grunt together who have never really even gotten to know each other on a friendship level, not to mention a father-son level. We'll grunt, we'll slap five, we'll do things together that are loud, fast, and dirty, and still have very little understanding of what makes the other person tick.

Society's idea of what a real man is — this elite, rambled personality in shining armor — has to be seen for what it really is. We need to see how much we have let that mentality influence us, whether we realized it or not. Otherwise, we will never see the need for getting close to our sons. We will think that as long as we grunt together, the empty, shallow, and hollow relationship we have is okay.

Maybe that is the way you were treated as you grew up with your dad. Dads have been acting this way for years. Very few sons have grown up with a wholesome relationship with their father, to where they feel they can share anything and look at their dad as their best friend. That ought to be the goal of parenting our sons — to be viewed as their best friend.

If your dad treated you coldly, didn't have time for you, didn't connect with you heart-to-heart, or never really cried, laughed, and prayed with you, then it is only natural you have passed on that kind of relationship to your own son. Most of us learn our parenting skills from our own parents. Whatever they did to us, we end up doing inadvertently to our own kids, no matter how much we say we don't want to be like our parents.

Just because that is the way we were raised does not mean it is the right way to raise our own children. It's time for us to change the course of how our family will be raised. It's time to find the right way to develop a wholesome relationship with our own sons and be determined to do it, no matter how hard it might seem, how out-of-the-ordinary it may be, or how different it is from the way we were raised.

Many of the principles for developing closeness with your son are the same as developing a relationship with your daughter. Begin to pray for him. Claim Malachi 4:6, **He will turn the hearts of the fathers to their children, and the hearts of the children to their fathers.**

God will draw your heart close to your son. Don't just go through the motions of trying to be close, but really, genuinely care about what is going on in his life. Earnestly pray for him to be a man of God. Ask God to give him an incredible dream to make a difference in this world. Pray for God to be his confidence and the basis for his self-esteem, rather than feel the need to try to be "macho" according to the world's standard.

Are you being a true spiritual father to your son? Remember, you are the priest of the house. Impart to him nuggets of what it takes to be a man of God. Show him scriptures on being a real man. Teach him about character and integrity. Does your son look up to you spiritually, or are you just the breadwinner?

In too many homes across America and around the world, the spiritual leader is the mother. She is the one who gets the children to church and who teaches Scripture verses. We dads need to be the ones who do that. This image goes against the popular image of being a man — that you're macho, and you're not touchy, feely.

But a real man is humble. Jesus is the only "real man" who ever lived. He showed us the example of being humble before His Father and being a servant towards others. If you want your son to grow to be a real man, you need to be the example of a real man — a spiritual father teaching him principles on which to build his life.

Remember, you are an example of the Father God. What he sees in you is what he will think the Father God, Whom he can't see, is like. In addition, the kind of father you are to him is the kind of father he will be to his children. You can create an incredible legacy now by representing your Father God in an accurate way and passing down an example that he in turn will live for his children, and they their children.

Is there anything you have done to push him away from you, whether purposely or inadvertently? Most of us would not do things on purpose to push our sons away, but there are things we do repeatedly that we know every time we do them we feel them slip further away. Yet we continue to do it.

Many fathers make the mistake of demanding so much from their son, he can never live up to the father's expectations. He's always behind the eight ball. No matter how good he does, he could always do better. He never feels approval or acceptance from his dad. He carries this around with him like a black cloud his whole life.

Many fathers have committed a sin of omission. They have omitted talking to their sons. They have not really shared their heart or taken a chance to get close. They've never cried in front of their sons. Does that make you a real man if you do cry? No. But if you are really hurting, it's okay to cry. *It's about being yourself.* It's about sharing who you are. It means taking time to sit down and talk with him.

What is your son really thinking and feeling? If you haven't done this over the years, you have no doubt created an air of anger, resentment, and coldness. Your son has wanted someone he can share his heart with and talk with. Every time he's tried — and if it ever got a little emotionally intense — he got a "Well, how about those Bears?" Rather than dealing with feelings and being straight-up honest with each other, you talk about sports or something on a superficial level.

These are just a few things that may have built a wall between you and your son. Blast through that wall by asking your son to forgive you. Be humble about it. Turn over a new leaf. Go against the grain of what society says a real man is. This will be the starting point of an incredible relationship between you and your son.

CHAPTER SEVEN . . . **WHAT TO DO IF YOU ARE A DAD WHO WANTS TO DEVELOP A CLOSE RELATIONSHIP WITH YOUR SON**

Let's talk about showing your son wholesome affection. What?! Is there such a thing as wholesome affection from one man to another man?! Of course there is. When God created the family with both a mother and a father, He knew it would take guidance, attention, input, and affection from both a male and a female for a young person to grow in a wholesome environment.

The problem is that most of us men have never been shown wholesome affection. We don't know what it looks like. We think any kind of affection from one man to another man is something seen only in the homosexual lifestyle, so we stay far away from that.

But we are not only emotional and spiritual beings — we are physical beings. And physical affection between a father and son is wholesome. I can't tell you how many young men — teenage guys — I've talked to who tell me, "My dad has never told me he loves me. My dad has never hugged me. I just wish my dad would give me a big bear hug." Start putting your arm around your son and letting him know he's important to you.

"As a boy grows and becomes older, his need for physical affection such as hugging and kissing lessens, but his need for physical contact does not. Instead of baby 'love stuff,' he needs 'boy-style' physical contact, such as bear hugs, 'give-me-five' hand slaps, and old-fashioned roughhousing."[3]

"Not all touches need to be physical to be effective," says William Beausay II, in his book *Boys! Shaping Ordinary Boys into Extraordinary Men.* Beausay says a dad can touch his son by:

1. Asking his opinion

2. Repeating his exact words after him

3. Putting up a "welcome home" banner on the house after school

4. Saying a poem with his name in it

5. Splitting a bag of candy with him right before dinner

6. Dropping everything and listening to him[4]

Tell him you love him. Don't assume he knows it. Tell him! It doesn't matter if he's 17 years old, hug his neck if he did something great. Put your arm around him when he is going through a struggle. Too many men would pass that off with, "Real men don't cry. Just get over it." As a result we pass along the legacy of coldness.

All too often, young men who don't get proper affection from their fathers, end up looking for approval or affection from another male and end up in a homosexual lifestyle. When they didn't get the wholesome kind of affection, they turned to the unwholesome affection because it satisfied their longing for attention.

Get over this idea that says you're not a real man if you hug your son. Tell him you love him. Too many of our sons are hurting and crying out on the inside, and we are buried in a shallow facade of machoism, too afraid to tell them we love them because our fathers never told us. It's time to be real. It's time to be honest.

Take off the mask, look your son in the eye, and say, "I love you, son."

8

What to do if you are divorced and your young person is in the custody of your ex-spouse

It must be one of the hardest scenarios a parent faces today — wanting to be the right influence over your young person, yet not having total control over the forces that influence them, even in the context of your own home. You have been through the battle of the divorce, the hurt and pain of separation from your spouse, and the hurt and pain of separation between you and your teen. Now they are in the heat of their teenage years when they need you the most. Some of the toughest situations they will ever face are on the horizon and they need your guidance and counsel. You are not afforded much of an opportunity to speak into those situations, which is complicated by the fact that most ex-spouses do not get along very well.

Teens all over the nation are feeling the effects of divorce:

"I wish that when my mom talked to me she would say 'dad' like she used to when they were together. Instead she says, 'your dad' which makes it seems like she has nothing to do with him."

"When my parents got divorced they never explained to me why. I'm in custody of my mom and now my dad is giving me guilt trips about not staying at his house more often. I wish he would understand that I just like staying with my mom better."

"My mom talked bad about my dad through the divorce. They treated each other with no respect around their children."

"They yelled about the other parent when they were just as much to blame and made me choose who to live with."

"I moved in with my dad because I fought with my mom. I wish they would have learned to communicate with each other better and therefore prevent this."

In *Smart Money* (September, 1995), the United States is cited as the major industrialized country with the highest divorce rate. Divorce has taken its toll on the young people of this generation.[1] Josh McDowell lists the effects of divorce as denial, shame/embarrassment, blame/guilt, anger, fear, relief, insecurity/low self-esteem, grief, depression, alienation and loneliness, academic problems, behavioral problems, sexual activity, substance abuse, and suicide threats and attempts.[2]

Maybe you have partial custody of your teenager — part of the time they are with you and part of the time they are with their father or mother. Maybe you see them on weekends, every other week, or every six months. You can see that no matter how many letters you write or how many phone calls you make, it doesn't seem to do much good, so you are tempted to just cut everything off.

In *Counseling Families After Divorce,* David R. Miller, Ph.D., gives the following suggestions:

1. Assist noncustodial parents to control, reduce, or eliminate emotional reactions. This can be accomplished most readily by listening uncritically and through validating the feelings being expressed.

2. Assist noncustodial parents to accept the reality of their situation. Specifically:

   a. They are in a position that discounts the parental role.

   b. The court has the power to award custody, determine visitation, and order child support payments.

   c. There are consequences of disobeying court orders, regardless of their feelings or whether they are permitted to see their children.

   d. The award of custody and determination of visitation are usually permanent and irreversible.

3. Assist noncustodial parents to stop behaving in self-defeating ways.

4. Assist noncustodial parents in realistically assessing their situation and negotiating an effective level of parental involvement without custody."[3]

What exactly is a parent do in this particularly difficult situation?

> **Children, obey your parents in the Lord, for this is right. "Honor your father and mother" — which is the first commandment with a promise — "that it may go well with you and that you may enjoy long life on the earth."**
>
> Ephesians 6:1-3

Now obviously this is a commandment to young people from the Lord to honor their mother and their father, to esteem them highly, to look up to them, to listen to them, and to treat them with respect. Sometimes, as a result of the divorce, we make it difficult for our teen to respect and honor the other parent through things we say, comments we make, or stories we tell.

The best situation for your teen to be in is for them to be honoring their mother and father. The problem, however, is that we get jealous. We don't want our teen to honor and respect the other parent more than they honor and respect us, so we tear the other one down, thinking they will like us more. We see our own interests as more important than the interests of the young person.

Your teen needs to honor their parents. You can help by not telling them every story of hurt that happened or everything your spouse did or said. You need to protect your ex-spouse and make them look good even when they may not deserve it. Why? Because you are protecting your teen.

CHAPTER EIGHT . . . **WHAT TO DO IF YOU ARE DIVORCED AND YOUR YOUNG PERSON IS IN THE CUSTODY OF YOUR EX-SPOUSE**

Like it or not, your ex-spouse is still the mother or father of your child. When divorced persons play the childish game of being jealous for the attention and respect of their young person, it ends up doing the young person a lot more harm. It rips their heart apart. It rips their allegiance apart. Sometimes they believe you, sometimes they believe the other one.

That is one reason God hates divorce. (See Malachi 2:16.) He knows it rips apart the hearts of those getting divorced as well as the hearts of the children. Making the best out of a terrible situation helps them respect both parents. It's bad enough there has been a divorce, but you further drag their heart down a bumpy road of pain, remorse, and regret, continually reminding them their parents are not married, by constantly slamming your ex-spouse.

If you have said or done anything like that, as I'm sure all divorced persons have done from time to time (I know my parents did it all the time), ask your young person to forgive you. "I'm sorry for what I said about your dad. Even though I may not like him and we had our own reasons for divorce, I had no right to drag down your estimation of him."

This takes humility. It takes a man or woman who is big on the inside to humble themselves and choose not to be threatened if the other parent looks good. In the long run, you are the one who will look good, because your young person will look back on the fact that you did not try to tear their heart away from the other parent. That says you are mature and secure and not intimidated by someone else's success or respect.

"Although parents see remarriage as a positive move, children often don't. They especially experience the fact that stepfamilies are born of loss. Studies show that being in a stepfamily is a risk factor for problems from dropping out of school to child abuse. Stepchildren are twice as likely to have behavioral problems as kids in nuclear families."[4]

Talk to your ex-spouse about agreeing on issues for the sake of your children. For example, agree on how you refer to each other and how you talk about each other (what we just discussed). Don't ask them to constantly give you honor, but say, "Listen, I've decided that whenever I refer to you to our son or daughter, I am only going to say good things. We have had our differences and we made mistakes, but that is all behind us. We may not like each other, but you are still my son's mother or father and I am going to afford you the respect you deserve because you hold that position."

That could be the starting point of the most wholesome kind of parenting that can take place between divorced parents. Then see if your ex-spouse will reciprocate the same kind of overture. They may or may not. They may want to see if you are serious about it before they do it. Don't let that inhibit you from doing what is right.

Agree on the rules you establish for your young person. So much dissension happens between a teen and their parents because, "Mom always lets me do this," and "Dad always lets me do that." The parents compete with each other to see how much fun they can let the kid have when they are at their house, hoping they will like them more and want to be with them more than the other parent. The competition between parents to see who can have the most fun is detrimental for the young person. It becomes a political game between the two ex-spouses, and the best interest of the young person is not considered at all.

CHAPTER EIGHT . . . **WHAT TO DO IF YOU ARE DIVORCED AND YOUR YOUNG PERSON IS IN THE CUSTODY OF YOUR EX-SPOUSE**

Talk through what is permitted and what is not, what kind of movies your teen can watch, and how late they can stay out. Commit to find some sort of middle ground on those areas you disagree on for the sake of your young person. It is not important — or even about — who they like the most. They will be the healthiest if there is consistency between the two of you.

In addition, if there is a stepparent involved, the rules should always be enforced by the biological parent, not the stepparent. You never want the young person to respond to correction with, "Well, you're not my real parent anyway."

Sometimes a stepfather is called upon to enforce the rules for a son or daughter who is not their own because they are the man of the house. Although that is true, there is still a role that a biological parent has that a stepparent doesn't get naturally. The stepparent needs to earn that role, respect, and right. They don't get it simply because of who they married.

Agree about gifts — how much money you will spend on gifts and what each of you will get your young person for Christmas, birthdays, or other special holidays. If it is possible to have any kind of agreement on this, it will be much easier for the young person. Again, you are not in competition about who can be the best parent and get the best gifts so the young person will like you more. It is about what is best for the young person.

What do they really need? How much is too much? How much will make them materialistic, self-centered, and feel like they always get whatever they want? Agree that you won't compete with each other, but that you will look beyond your own desires and needs to the needs of the young person.

Any time your child visits one of the parents, the child should not be showered with gifts the other spouse cannot afford. In such case, it would be noble for the parent who can afford it to give money to the parent who cannot afford it so there is equal exchange of gifts. Then the son or daughter doesn't grow up thinking one parent is better than the other because they give them more "stuff."

Another challenge you might face is the child playing one parent against the other. "Mom let's me do it," or "Dad let's me do it." Comments like that will make you want to be competitive with each other. But if you are on the same wavelength and in agreement on these issues, it will be almost impossible for your young person to manipulate you into that kind of situation.

If you do hear those remarks, stop them by saying, "We'll talk about it later." Then make a phone call to your ex-spouse. "Hey, is this something we haven't talked about that we need to come into agreement on?"

If your young person knows they can't play you against one another, the competition will be defused rather than fueled. If your teen senses they can fuel it, you know they will. As a result, your young person will have a much better relationship with you and your ex-spouse, you will have at least a marginally pleasant and agreeable relationship with your former spouse, and your young person will be all the better for it.

9

What to do if your teen has no idea what to do with their life — no vision

Where there is no vision, the people perish.

Proverbs 29:18 KJV

Without a vision, the people are destroyed, aimless, confused, bewildered, and directionless. This describes much of what this generation of young people is like.

> "I didn't have a job, so my mom just yelled at me and told me I was lazy and would never get a job."

> "My parents need to encourage me and tell me to press on with my goals."

Many parents feel sad that their own young person does not have direction, but they don't quite know what to do about it. They figure that somehow, some way, their young person will figure out on their own what they should do with their life. They graduate from high school and go through one door at a time, trying to find their way along the path of life. Seventeen-year-old Brooke Davidoff said, "About one-third of our generation doesn't care about anything important. It's kind of like anything goes."[1] "More than 98 percent of teens ages 13-17 say it's at least somewhat likely that they will have good-paying jobs as adults, and more than six in ten think that there is some likelihood they may be rich someday. Yet almost half say they are likely to be mugged, and 33 percent believe they may be shot or stabbed in their lifetime.[2]

According to *USA Today's* poll of 703 high school student leaders, marriage is slightly more important than career. In looking to the future, 31.5 percent are looking forward to a successful marriage; 28.9 percent to a successful career; 20.9 percent to acquiring knowledge; 14.4 percent to making money; and 4.3 percent to raising children. Job satisfaction is the most important thing in a job according to 65.5 percent; 29.8 percent said money was; and 4.7 percent said that prestige was.[3]

As a parent, one of our goals should be to raise our children to be morally and socially responsible. They will do the right thing even after they have left the supervision of our home because of what has been instilled in them during their upbringing. Part of raising a responsible young person is helping them to know what to do with their life and helping them to sort out the myriad of options.

Some parents want their children to live out their dreams. They want their children to accomplish what they were never able to accomplish themselves. So they have always told their young person, "You are going to be a doctor," or "You are going to be a lawyer." Setting aside all of our personal biases and opinions, we need to look at the young person's utmost good and help them discover what God's plan is for *their* life. This can be frustrating for us if *we* never sought to find God's will for *our* life when we were young. Some of us have a hard time even now trying to find out what the Lord wants us to do.

You would be surprised at how much your young person actually wants you to be involved in helping them discover what is right for their life. As one teen put it,

> "I wish my parents cared about what I wanted to do with my life; but they keep trying to kill my dreams."

Whatever you do, be careful not to be a dream-killer. There are so many parents who have discouraged their young person by things they have said to them. The young person will mention an idea and they will respond with, "Oh, you will never do that," or "You can never become that," or "You will probably be flipping burgers your whole life." Even though these things may be said in jest or be off-the-cuff comments, the damage they can do to a young person's dreams is not only destructive, but often eternal.

Without a doubt, as you begin to talk to your young person about their desires and dreams for the future, they will come up with ideas and dreams that might sound far-fetched, way beyond their ability, or way beyond your desire for them to go that direction. You must remember, though, that it is *their* life, not yours. It is our parental responsibility to help our young people. Rather than letting them do whatever they can do and coming up with whatever they can come up with, we should help them discover their dreams and develop a vision for their lives.

FUTURE

Another equally important goal is to help your young person find out what God's best is for their life. Many people have never considered what God's plan might be. Yet there is something about important decisions like what college to go to and who to marry that makes everyone wonder "Is this really the right thing?" You can only measure whether it is right or not by knowing the One who made you and knowing all the potential He put inside you.

> **Before I formed you in the womb I knew you, before you were born I set you apart; I appointed you as a prophet to the nations.**

> **Jeremiah 1:5**

Before we were ever conceived God knew who we were, what our gifts were going to be, all the potential He put inside of us, and all the incredible things each of us could do to change the world and make it a better place.

Our responsibility is to help our young person realize the destiny God has placed on their life and the potential He has put inside them. We need to open our ears and hearts as well as help them to open theirs, so they can hear what God's plan is for their life.

The first step in knowing His plan is knowing Him. If you want to know the purpose for a piano, go talk to the one who made the piano. They will tell you why they made it and what it is to be used for. If we want to know the purpose of our lives, we need to go to our Maker and find out His plan for us.

Tom East, in *Vision and Challenge,* points out three ways you can enable young people to hear God's voice more clearly in their noisy world.

1. **Media literacy.** Professional attention-getters bombard teenagers with constant messages. When you help kids critique the media world in which they live, they're better able to understand these influences and the choices they present. This can help them focus on God's call.

2. **Reflection.** Teenagers need space to reflect on the direction their lives are taking. Silence is an important part of learning to pay attention. You can help kids by building pauses and short periods of silence into programs. Be sure to help them make connections between their beliefs and their actions.

3. **A spiritually challenging vision of life.** Give teenagers lots of opportunities to see God's call lived out in others' lives. Communicate a broad vision to kids by introducing them to a variety of people who are living for Christ in everyday life.[4]

During this process, help your young person make a list of all the gifts and talents they have, all the things they have ever wanted to do with their life, and all the ideas and opinions others have had regarding what they should do with their life (i.e. fields that people have suggested they should go into). Most importantly, help your young person discover their convictions.

God has deposited convictions in our own hearts and lives, and we often do not search deep inside enough to know what those

FUTURE

are. A conviction is something you feel so strongly about that if you do not do it, you know you will be miserable for the rest of your life. You can have convictions such as, "I must work in the medical field," or "I must help people in some way," or "I must work in another country as a missionary."

Begin a dialogue with your young person. Discuss these kinds of things with them and meet once a month during their high school years to add to their list or take things off the list. You will see how things are refined after a number of years or months of going through this kind of process.

Spend time praying over each one of the things on the list. Consider talking to people who are specialists in some of the areas your young person is interested in. You won't have all the answers for them, and you shouldn't tell them what to do with their life. But letting your young person know you are interested and helping them walk through the milieu of confusion and options they are facing will let them know you care.

To reinforce their sense of purpose and destiny, help your teen write down their vision for life.

Write down the revelation [vision] and make it plain on tablets so that a herald may run with it.

Habakkuk 2:2

After seeking and thinking through all the different possibilities, it is very important to have your young person write down a mini-plan. "This is where I'm going and this is how I'm going to get there" is the essence of this plan.

In a study of Harvard graduates, only 5 percent had written down their vision when they graduated. After 20 years, only that 5 percent had accomplished their vision and each were making an annual salary that totaled the combined income of the other 95 percent of their classmates'. Realize the importance of writing down your vision!

By walking down this road with our young person, we hope to see them launch into the direction in life they are best suited for. We can watch them accomplish all the dreams God has placed in their heart and become a success in whatever field they are destined to go into.

FUTURE

10

What to do if your teen is having a hard time choosing a college

It stands to reason that if a young person desires to go to college, they should first have an idea of the direction they want to go. If your young person is trying to choose a college and has not yet discovered a vision for their life, read chapter nine. Walk through that process with them before they choose a college.

So many teens struggle with the decision of what college to go to.

"It seems as though I have too many options. With so many options, it is hard for me to choose."

"I wish we would have started planning for college or praying about it earlier. I feel like I don't know where God would want me to go or to do."

"I wish my parents would say, 'Let God be your guide; not money or your own mind-set. God has a greater plan for you'."

If your teen does have a direction or somewhat of a vision of what they want to do with their life, the first question to ask regarding a college would be, "Where is the best place for them to go to become an expert in this area?" The first question should not be, "Can we afford a particular school?"

Research schools that would best equip them, regardless of finances. When looking for a college, cost is uppermost in students' minds. These are some of the other major deciding factors:

1. Cost: 33.5 percent

2. Academics: 25.6 percent

3. Location: 20.6 percent

4. Friends: 12.8 percent

5. Prestige: 7.5 percent[1]

Finances come in a number of different ways, but the first thing to do is set up your young person for success. Do not consider schools because they are close to home or far from home, or where their brothers, sisters, or you went to school. Some characteristics college freshmen say were very important in helping them select the college they now attend are:

1. It has a good academic reputation: 56.1 percent

2. Its graduates get good jobs: 47.5 percent

3. Its graduates go to top graduate schools: 27.5 percent

4. It has a good social reputation: 26.7 percent

5. It offers special programs: 22 percent

6. It has low tuition: 20.9 percent

7. It offers financial assistance: 20.2 percent

8. Students want to live near home: 17.9 percent[2]

Begin researching various schools. Look at degree plans at the university your teen is considering. What classes would your teen be required to take? Study those classes to see what they would actually learn by taking them, not just what the title of the classes are. Don't count on a school just because it has a major in your teen's particular area — talk to the professors or to graduates who have gone through the program your teen is considering. What did they really learn? What are they doing with what they learned? Just because a school has a program in a certain area does not mean it is preparing students for success.

For example, there are some theological seminaries that teach courses on how to be a pastor or youth pastor, or how to preach. They have a whole curriculum developed around these areas, yet many of the professors have never been a pastor or a youth pastor, or have never preached. This would be like a doctor in medical school lecturing on how to do brain surgery, yet never having performed it himself. That is ridiculous!

Graduates of the program would be able to share what they got out of it, and what it is producing in their lives. Talk to some of the current students at the school as well. College is like a greenhouse or an incubator in terms of attitude and probability for success. What is the *environment* of the campus?

FUTURE

Some might say, "Why go to college? Is everyone designed for college?" Jesus said in Luke 14:28-30, "**Suppose one of you wants to build a tower. Will he not first sit down and estimate the cost to see if he has enough money to complete it? For if he lays the foundation and is not able to finish it, everyone who sees it will ridicule him, saying, 'This fellow began to build and was not able to finish.'**"

The same is true of your young person's vision. They have these great visions, dreams, and goals, yet they have not really thought about what it takes to fulfill them. So many people talk hot air their whole life. They want to do this and they want to do that — but they never do anything. They don't count the cost, they don't prepare, and they don't build.

Finding the right college is like counting the cost in building a tower. It is doing the preparation work in order for that tower to stand for a long time. The tower your teen is building is their life. If you want to help them achieve success, help them count the cost and know what it will take to build their life with success. What environment will thrust them to the front lines of excellence?

Young people who are considering doing something in the ministry face the choice of Bible school or college. A Bible school teaches you *what* to think and *what* to believe. Students take classes that train them in a particular way of thinking or a particular kind of theology. A college teaches you *how* to think. It blasts you with a myriad of different options and theories so you learn how to process them and how to think through them. As a result, you have not been programmed on a certain way of thinking or believing, but you have learned how to process and think through issues.

I believe a lot more young people are suited for college than most believe. God gave us a brain to use and to develop. If we do not develop ourselves, we are ripping ourselves off. If we do not encourage our young people to develop themselves, they are getting ripped off. Their potential, and what they could accomplish with their life, is being compromised from the very beginning.

I have seen many young people go to college who were total goof-offs in high school. They never thought they were cut out for college and certainly never thought they could make it in college. They never thought they could afford it and never had any interest in going. However, they ended up going and developing themselves, and went on to be very successful in different areas of life.

In a survey of 210,000 college freshmen, these were some important key factors in deciding to go to college:

1. Get a better job: 82.6 percent

2. Learn more about things: 72.4 percent

3. Make more money: 71.3 percent

4. Gain general education: 60.7 percent

5. Prepare for graduate school: 47.2 percent

6. Improve reading and study skills: 39.8 percent

7. Become a more cultured person: 33.5 percent

8. Parents wanted me to go: 17.3 percent

FUTURE

9. Wanted to get away from home: 10 percent

10. Could not find a job: 3.2 percent

11. Nothing better to do: 2.5 percent[3]

Is college meant for everyone? The goal of college is not just the education you receive, but learning how to think. Not everyone needs college in order to develop the ability to think and process information. I know only a handful of people who are excelling in life without college, but I believe they are the exception to the rule. I certainly do not fit into that category. I think most people do not. Everyone has the possibility of excelling, and most people need to get into an environment where they can be trained how to think and how to develop themselves. That is what college is for.

Some young people would say, "I want to take a year and work first, before I go to college," or "I just want to go to a community college and try to figure things out." If they are pushed to develop their vision when they are in high school, they ought to be able to jump right out of high school and into college with direction, rather than stumble through college trying to figure out what to major in.

If they get to the end of their high school career and do not yet know what they want to do with their lives, instead of stumbling through a year of college trying to figure it out or just working for a year, they ought to enlist themselves in a program that can help them develop their future and their potential.

The disadvantage of working for a year is that they set themselves up to lose their hope of going to college. They may lose their initiative or even get pulled into a relationship that prevents them from fulfilling their dream. Getting involved in a program such as the Teen Mania Internship can be most beneficial. Hundreds of young people come every year for a whole year of developing their character and vision for life. You can find more information about the Internship program by writing to the address at the back of this book.

Commit to the Lord whatever you do, and your plans will succeed.

Proverbs 16:3

Just because you are encouraging your young person to go to college does not mean you must pay out all the money. Once you have helped them select a college, there are a number of ways available to get your teen through school. There is more than $24 billion in financial aid available for students each year. Grants, such as the Pell Grant, and loans are available from the government. Your local library has a list of scholarship and grant opportunities available. There are also "800" numbers for firms that will research what grants or loans your young person may be qualified to receive. Start with the following sources, most of which can be found in your library:

How to Put Your Children Through College without Going Broke (New York: The Research Institute of America, Inc.)

The Scholarship Book. Daniel Cassidy and Michael J. Alves (Englewood Cliffs, New Jersey: Prentice Hall Publishers)

FUTURE

Directory of Financial Aid for Minorities and *Directory of Financial Aid for Women.* Gail Ann Schlachter, editor. (Redwood City, California: Reference Service Press)

Paying Less for College (Princeton, New Jersey: Peterson's Guides)

Winning Money for College. Alan Deutschman. (Princeton, New Jersey: Peterson's Guides)

Need a Lift? (Indianapolis, Indiana: The Américan Legion)

For information on the federal aid programs, call the Student Aid Information Center toll-free at (800) 433-3243.

For information on cooperative education, write to: The National Commission for Cooperative Education, 360 Huntington Ave., Boston, Massachusetts 02115.[4]

Young people can also do it the old-fashioned way and work their way through school. I think a combination of these methods works the best. They should not go only on loans, grants, or money from their parents. Working while in school definitely teaches you discipline!

My parents were not able to help financially with my college education, and I ended up graduating in three and one-half years with a double major — and not one loan. My parents had not even graduated from high school, much less college. If I can make it through school, coming from a background where college was not really encouraged, not to mention paid for, surely there is not a young person in this country who could not do the same.

11

What to do if your teen listens to secular music

So many young people, even those who go to church, say things like this:

> "I love secular rock music. I am addicted to groups such as The Offspring and Nirvana."

> "I have no desire to quit listening to secular music. It affects me in no other way, but emotionally."

> "I listen to rock music and my parents like oldies. They are not Christian songs, but they consist of good music. I am intelligent and I do not believe that just because I don't listen to Christian music, I have a problem. I have no problem. I listen to music that I like, and I don't really have a liking for Christian music."

> "I don't think I would have started listening to secular music if my parents had home-schooled me or at least told me it was bad."

So many parents' attitudes are:

> "I cannot stop them anyway. They are going to do what they want to do when they are not with me."

"I have listened to secular music my whole life; and I am not that bad of a person."

Secular music today is much worse than it was when most of us were growing up. So much of a young person's identity comes from the kind of music they listen to. It reflects the kind of friends a young person hangs out with, mostly those who listen to that same style of music. Young people are drawn into a whole subculture according to the kind of music they listen to.

Some listen to it only occasionally. Others are obsessed, constantly having their headphones on, walking around in "another world," and watching MTV. Their philosophy of life and method of interaction with other people is dictated by the music they are listening to.

Musicians have been called "modern-day philosophers." If they sing songs about rebellion or that nothing but having fun and getting high really matters, then that becomes the philosophy of the day. Musicians have the power to shape society and the thought patterns of young people.

The impact of music and media on young people today is unprecedented. Quentin Schultze says, "In this type of adolescent culture, where identities are up for grabs and where adult-adolescent communication is weak, the media plays an unprecedented role in teenage life. First, the media challenges the authority of parents, pastors, and teachers. Teens look to media celebrities for styles of dress, acceptable behavior, and even values and beliefs to guide their lives. Rock-music stars, television characters and radio personalities are mentors and teachers, not just entertainers."[1]

James Dobson says, "It is difficult to overestimate the negative impact music is having. Rock stars are heroes, the idols, that young people want to emulate. And when they are depicted in violent and sexual roles, many teenagers and preadolescents are pulled along in their wake."[2]

Soundscan's Mike Shalett said, "Every generation needs music that screams rebellion to parents. Alternative did that, but it was quickly co-opted. Now labels need to provide some kind of rebellious, anthemic music that the young consumer can call their own." A special subcommittee of the American Medical Association reports that the average teenager listens to 10,500 hours of rock music between the seventh and twelfth grades.[3]

What do you do if your young person has been sucked into this?

Don't come right out and say, "We are never having that music again in our house!" Your young person may not listen to it in the house, but they may still be listening to it outside the home. Remember, your teen is a young adult — they are not a child anymore. The wise thing is to create a dialogue with them that will make them want to put *their* foot down and not just stop listening to it because you say so. However, there is some music that is so vile and so incredibly satanic, such as Marilyn Manson, that you have to put your foot down, whether they understand your reason for doing so or not.

Find out more about the musical groups they are interested in. Do some research and find interviews with these groups so you can know more about what they stand for and represent. You can start with *Rolling Stone* or *Spin* magazines. Show them to your teenager. Study the lyrics together. Read the interviews

MUSIC AND MEDIA

together. "Let's look at these and see what these bands are really like. What have they done with their lives? What kind of lifestyles do they lead? Are these people who you really want influencing your life?"

In doing so you will be teaching them how to make a wise decision for themselves, rather than just saying, "Do not listen to it because I say so." At the very least, show your teen you are informed and interested, that your recommendation not to listen is for legitimate, logical reasons, not that you simply don't like it.

Show them you care enough about what they are doing to be involved with them. Psalm 101:3 says, **I will set before my eyes no vile thing.** That is, "I do not want to be near anything that could possibly take me away from God or put garbage into my life, because I know it could wreck me." So many young people say, "I don't listen to the words, I just listen to the music. It won't influence me because I don't listen to the words. I am a coherent human being. I know not to go out and do the things they are talking about. They are just a popular group." On the contrary, the lyrics *do* influence their minds and the way they think, whether they believe it or not.

The spiritual implications of listening to secular music are incredible. The majority of secular musicians do not have high standards or ethics in their lives. Most of them drink and are involved in drug abuse. (Chapter 17 goes into the spiritual ramifications of what happens when someone is involved with drugs.)

Often these bands, trying to be creative, write their music after getting drunk or high on drugs. Because they have given the control of their mind over to a drug, they have opened themselves to demonic influence. They have opened themselves to evil spirits, spirits of depression, spirits of oppression, and every kind of confusion imaginable.

The group comes up with lyrics, sings the song, and puts it on a CD. Now your good, church-going young person, who loves the Lord but likes listening to secular music, hears it. They never had any desire to do drugs, drink, or be involved with the devil, but because they are pumping this music into their brain, they are hearing someone who has been influenced by the demonic world. The music may be blatantly rebellious as they "sing about the devil," or it may have more subtle lyrics — but it feeds your teen total depression.

The spirit of the musician is infused into the spirit and the heart of the young person listening to that musician. Young people can get the same demonic oppression without being on drugs or alcohol, because they are getting it directly from the person who created and produced these songs — inspired by the enemy of our souls.

"What about love songs?" your teen may ask. Love songs are not wrong if they are inspired by God's love. But if they are inspired by the world's viewpoint and the enemy's perspective, they'll have a skewed version of what love is. Young people listening to them will end up with the most confused ideas on love and what a wholesome relationship is all about.

Saying, "Now boys and girls, don't listen to that music because it will hurt you," will do no good. Your young person is being invaded by the world of the enemy and doesn't even know it. They are opening themselves up to the world of darkness

MUSIC AND MEDIA

with the reasoning, "Everyone else is listening to this band. It's not that bad." For the sake of your young person and their spiritual and emotional survival, help them to understand the ramifications.

> **Finally, brothers, whatever is true, whatever is noble, whatever is right, whatever is pure, whatever is lovely, whatever is admirable — if anything is excellent or praiseworthy — think about such things.**
>
> **Philippians 4:8**

There is nothing inherently wrong with a particular style of music, whether it is rock and roll, rap, or big band. What is more important is the spirit and attitude behind the musician singing or writing the music. Instrumental music has no words to convey the spirit and the heart of the musician, but no matter what style of music it is, if it is not written and performed by those with a pure heart and mind, it will take your teen down the wrong path. As they hear the words, it conveys the attitude and perspective of someone without God in the center of their life.

Why in the world would anyone who wants to live a reputable and upright life, with God in the center, want to be influenced by someone living a life without God? Help your young person see it that way, rather than just telling them not to listen to it because it's wrong. Help them to see the lifestyles of the singers and bands. Show them they are singing about life from a perspective that is dark, depraved, and at the very least, without God.

12

What to do if your young person is obsessed with weird or wild Christian rock music

First of all, be glad that it is *Christian* music. Rejoice in the fact that they are not obsessed with weird or wild *secular* music. But, still you are concerned. Your teen is dressing strangely, dancing in weird ways, hitting their head against the wall or bobbing it up and down, jumping up and down, making strange noises, or going to all sorts of concerts. Next, you hear about the moshing that goes on there. Your teen is wanting to go see bands with weird names you have never heard of before, but who claim to be Christian groups.

What is a parent to do? First of all, what not to do is sit by blindly thinking, "Well, at least they are Christian groups." Don't let your young person listen to whatever they want to listen to and go wherever they want to go. It is your responsibility as a parent to make sure that even though a band or an activity has a Christian label on it, you are doing all you can to be the chief guiding force in your young person's life. You cannot let peers, music, news, or teachers be their primary guiding force. God has put *you* there to train them, not the music industry nor the educational system.

What can you do to help guide them through this? Ask your young person to let you see the lyrics to some songs. Sit down together and look over them. If there are lyrics you do not understand, ask your young person what they mean. Compare them to scriptures to see if they really line up with the Word of God. Read magazine articles about the bands. Find interviews with them and read them with your young person. See what the band members are like. How long have they been Christians? Where do they go to church? Do they have a regular pastor? Are they accountable to anyone?

In regards to music and your teen, does the word *obsessed* come to mind? The word *obsessed* is a big word. It means your teen *has* to listen to it all the time — sunup to sundown. They can't stand to be without it. It's amazing the strong pull that music has on our society. If your young person is so compelled that they cannot stay away, then there is something wrong. If they need to constantly have their headphones on with the CD player going, that is evidence that something is not right. It's one thing to like that kind of music, but it is another thing to be so sucked into it that it is all they can think about, and all they ever want to do.

The fallacy is to think, "Well, when they are not with us, we don't have any control over them anyway. We might as well let them listen to it as much as they want. It's Christian — it won't harm them." That is not necessarily so. Just because it is Christian music does not mean that it is healthy for a young mind to be bombarded with fast-paced, crazy guitars screaming through their headphones all day long. It breeds confusion in their heart and mind. Keep in mind that if you tell your young person this, they won't believe it, understand it, or agree with it.

The second fallacy is that you do not have any influence. Yes you do! You are the parent. You are the one who is there to say what is wise and what is not — what is permissible and what is not. You can limit how much time your teen spends listening to a CD player or Walkman by telling them you don't think it is wise for them to listen to that style of music all day long. Suggest that they listen to some praise and worship or teaching tapes. Maybe they need some quiet time without constant noise broadcast into their brain all day. You do have influence. You are there to set guidelines and parameters so your teen will be raised in a wholesome environment. Do your job.

Listening to this kind of music is a cultural belonging thing. Young people will get around other young people who listen to the same music, want to dress the same way, etc. Instead of dwelling on "Why do you listen to this?" dive into who your teen's friends are. Who are they hanging out with? Who are they going to the concerts with?

Young people are desperately looking for some kind of belonging, and they find it in a group of other young people who listen to the same music they do, have the same attitude, talk the same way, and dress the same way. When they find a place of belonging, they will be committed to it. It is important for you to be involved with the group your young person finds their belonging with. Help them find the right friends and belong to the right kind of group.

Even if they like a good band whose lyrics are biblically sound, it does not mean you should let your young person listen to it

MUSIC AND MEDIA

all the time. Too much of anything can be harmful — and it is the same with wild Christian music. Be careful. Many of the bands are not mature in the Lord. They have talent, have given their lives to the Lord, and are now using their talent to sing about Jesus. However, they could be very shallow and could ultimately lead your young person into a not-so-good situation.

In examining the lyrics, be sure they agree with the whole counsel of Scripture. Encourage your young person to find out enough about the group (through interviews and articles) to know a little about their lifestyle. This will give you a greater confidence in both the lyrics and the lifestyles of the band members. The bands your young person is listening to should be a positive influence and leave them with correct and sound theology.

13

What to do if your teen is watching too much TV

It seems like every time you walk into the living room, the television is on and your teen is sitting around, flipping through the channels to find the hottest program. You walk into their bedroom — the television is on, their headphones are in their ears, or they're staring at the computer screen. You try to start up some kind of conversation and their response is, "Yeah, yeah...as soon as I'm done with this."

We have such a media-craved, media-controlled society that it has diverted attention away from interaction and personal relationships with parents and friends. If people can't get along, can't work out a situation, or are just tired of being with people, it's easy to retreat to a machine — something they don't have to argue with, that won't talk back to them, and something they can enjoy.

Instead of having a relationship with a person, they have a relationship with a video screen. They have a difficult time with friendships, with friendships of the opposite sex that could develop into marriage, and with family relationships. They don't have to work things out — they can just shut things out. Turn up the volume. Rent another movie. Watch another television program. Because they are totally absorbed in some kind of media, our young people are finding it difficult to develop wholesome relationships. In addition, they are also receiving much of their philosophy of life through music, television, and movies.

The question is, "How much is too much?" It's probably unrealistic to think your young person will actually shut the television off and never turn it back on. But where should parents draw the line? How can you draw the line in a way that is palatable to everyone and makes sense to your young person?

The typical American household has a television on seven hours a day. Teenagers watch approximately 21 hours of TV a week.[1] Watching television is cited as the favorite leisure activity among teenagers, with 80 percent of those surveyed saying they watch television during their leisure time. Teenagers are the people with the most amount of leisure time at their discretion.[2]

About 50 percent of all teenagers have a television in their rooms.[3] The "family hour" — between 8 P.M. and 9 P.M. — is the most violent hour of television programming, with as many as 168 violent acts each week.[4] So much television-watching robs the family of opportunities for interaction with each other.

Bob Keeshhan, of *Captain Kangaroo* fame, says, "Television is really part of the extended family now in people's homes. It's right in the living room. Ninety-nine percent of parents don't care what their children watch on television because the parents use it as a baby-sitter."[5] Even among teenagers, as long as we know they are not getting in trouble, we don't really care what they are doing. We let television raise our young people and dictate their values.

Among the violent acts seen on television, 73 percent of the perpetrators go unpunished. Most violent portrayals do not show the consequences of a violent act — 47 percent show no harm to victims, 58 percent depict no pain, and only 16 percent show long-term consequences. Twenty-five percent of violent television incidents involve the use of handguns which, according to a study, can "trigger aggressive thoughts and behaviors."[6] Christian teens are more likely to watch MTV (42 percent) than their non-Christian peers (33 percent). The typical teen will allocate roughly one quarter of their television attention — about 25 minutes a day — to MTV.[7]

"By graduation day, the average high school student has seen 18,000 murders in 22,000 hours of television viewing. According to studies done at the Annenburg School of Communications in Philadelphia, 55 percent of prime-time characters are involved in violent confrontations once a week."[8]

How does watching television affect families? It can disrupt communication among family members and negate socialization skills. Perspective is lost if kids are watching television shows alone with no parental input or discussion. As a result, kids are getting a distorted view of social reality. They view those 20,000 murders (before the age of 18) without parents helping them understand that murder is wrong.

Viewers consider television personalities, like news anchors or soap opera/sitcom actors, more like friends than people who are actually in their lives.[9] Even with all this television-watching and the availability of television in their rooms, 75 percent of teenagers say that if given a choice between television and family time, they would opt for family time.[10]

MUSIC AND MEDIA

Again, what is a parent to do? Be very aware of how much television your young person is watching, whether it is in their room, at a friend's house, or in the living room of your own home. Find out what is being fed into their heart and mind. Also be aware of what programs they are watching — not just their names, but what they are about. Remember, what your teen watches instills values into them, shaping them for their present and future life. It will either depress or inspire them, motivate or discourage them.

Take control of the influences affecting your young person. Do this very diplomatically, because up to this point they have had the run of the show. They could flip the channels as much as they wanted, going through the cable and satellite channels at their own discretion. If all of a sudden you come down hard and say, "No more TV!" or "You can only watch the news," they may very well react negatively.

You are going to have to show them your desire for an increased relationship with them. Let them know you desire to do more family activities together — to go out and actually experience adventure rather than just watch it. The statistic stated earlier that most young people would rather spend time with their family — if their family is willing.

Is their leisure/extracurricular time being flushed down the drain by the television, or are you designing character-building/relationship-building activities to enrich your family? When your young person reflects back on their growing-up years, what will they remember doing most with their leisure time? Will they remember staring blankly into the television for hours on end, or will they remember a series of things you implemented to help them grow and develop?

Decide what programs and/or movies you want to watch together. Sit down as a family and talk about what is right or wrong in the program. Talk about *why* it is right or wrong. Use these opportunities to instill character and teach lessons, as opposed to just sitting in front of the television and vegging out.

Think of how much television *you* watch and how absorbed *you* get. Monitor your own TV-watching habits. Do you sit there and respond, "Yes, Dear," or "No, Dear," to your teen without really listening? Are you asking your young person to quit watching so much television, yet you are absorbed in it yourself?

Psalm 101:3 says, **I will set before my eyes no vile thing.** Don't let anything that is going to corrupt you, distract you, or pull you away from God enter your heart or mind. Think about that on behalf of your young person. Have we let the media become a surrogate parent? Do we wonder, "How could my young person actually think or act like that? Where did they get that attitude from?" when all the while we have let the television come into our living room and kidnap their hearts and minds? Let's be the parents God wants us to be by actively helping to shape the perspective of our young people as they develop into young adults.

MUSIC AND MEDIA

14

What to do if your teenager thinks the Bible or church is boring

It's Sunday morning and you begin the same series of conversations, trying to figure out new, creative ways to get your teenager to church. They have told you so many times that they don't want to go, they hate going, and they never get anything out of it. They have all kinds of excuses why they don't want to go or why they think they shouldn't have to go.

You, being a good parent and wanting to raise them in the right way, demand that they go no matter what. You don't know what else to do, but you figure if you can at least get them to church, maybe something good will sink in. You are taking the right action by making them go. Yet, is there a wiser way to accomplish the same objective, or even a bigger objective?

According to a Nielsen Media Research, when asked what kids like least about Christianity, their number one response was *church*.[1]

"To their credit, teenagers are more focused on God than on the institutional church. Almost six out of ten of them say they want to be close to God; not quite four out of ten say they are anxious to be active participants in a church.... Half of all kids attend a church worship service each week. As might be expected, the older teenagers become, the less frequently they attend church services, declining from two-thirds of all 13-year-olds attending church each weekend to less than half of all 18-year-olds. The most astounding realization in this regard is that teenagers are more likely to attend a church service every week than are adults....It should not be surprising that most teens admit that the chances of their leaving the church are at least as good as the chances of staying. Only two out of every five teens (41 percent) say they are 'very likely' to attend a church once they leave home. Roughly as many (36 percent) said they may attend, and the remaining one-quarter (22 percent) said the chances are slim to none."[2]

Most people who drop out of church do so between 16 and 19 years of age. The top six main reasons are:

1. Part-time jobs conflict with church life.

2. They think church is irrelevant.

3. They feel they don't fit in.

4. Challenging church training programs usually cease or taper off at this age.

5. Church activities are boring.

6. They are going through a time of questioning and doubting.

CHAPTER FOURTEEN . . . WHAT TO DO IF YOUR TEENAGER THINKS THE BIBLE OR CHURCH IS BORING

Maybe you have felt relatively unsuccessful in conveying your faith, your beliefs, and your values to your young person. You are hoping that if you keep dragging them to church something will find its way into their heart. There are many young people who say things like, "I really do love God, I just do not like the church. I don't like the people there. There are too many hypocrites." The list goes on and on.

Do you find yourself in the middle of that frustration? What are you to do? This should go without saying, but pray! Stand in the gap. Find scriptures to stand on.

Train a child in the way he should go, and when he is old he will not turn from it.

Proverbs 22:6

As for me and my household, we will serve the Lord.

Joshua 24:15

I will pour out my Spirit on all people. Your sons and daughters will prophesy, your old men will dream dreams, your young men will see visions.

Joel 2:28

All your sons will be taught by the Lord, and great will be your children's peace.

Isaiah 54:13

Pray those verses over your young person. Pray, "In Jesus' name, they are going to be a man or woman of God. Soften their heart, Lord." Pray that a passionate love for God will explode in their heart as the Lord becomes the center of everything they are.

Ask yourself, and do your best to discern from your teen, whether or not your young person really knows the Lord. The question is not really whether they like church or not, but do they really know the Lord. Have they ever given their life to Jesus? Have they ever opened up their heart? Are they sold out to Him? A lot of us who have raised young people in church their whole lives just assume that it is so.

"They have always been a good person...They don't really get into trouble..." But do they really know the Lord? If they do not know the Lord, no wonder they think church and the Bible are boring. Don't just go and ask them, "Do you know the Lord?" Through a series of conversations you will be able to tell if the Lord is the center of their life. If He is not, fuel your prayer time praying for them that they would truly, genuinely surrender their entire life to the Lord.

Get them a Bible that is easy to understand. It is amazing how many young people have *King James Version* Bibles, or some other version they do not understand. I cannot tell you how many people I have talked to who tell me they read their Bible but it just doesn't make sense to them. They get bored with it and do not read it anymore. Some parents are so committed to the *King James Version* or some other complicated version because that's what their pastor uses. That's fine for the pastor, but he has been through theology school. He knows the Greek and Hebrew and can get the real meaning out of it. The *King*

James Version is not the original version that Peter and Paul read. They read it in a whole different language.

Let me recommend to you a brand-new translation called the *Contemporary English Version,* a youth study Bible version I helped to edit. It is a translation that puts the Bible into today's understandable words. The study aids will help your teen understand different passages of Scripture and give them insight on where to turn when they are struggling or challenged in certain areas.

Ask yourself if the church you are going to is boring. Maybe not for you, but is it for your young person? This is a tough question, but if you really want your teen on fire, you need to answer it honestly. Maybe they are sincerely trying to get something out of it, but they can't because it's all geared toward an older congregation. Maybe the church is even boring to you, but the thought of leaving hasn't even crossed your mind. You have been there so long, you know all the people, all your friends are there, or maybe you were raised in that church. It may be providing a great social outlet, but is your faith getting fed? Is it spiritually dry? Are you gaining wisdom each week to help you grow in the Lord? More importantly, is your young person being presented the Gospel in such a way that will help them to really grow in the Lord?

According to a survey of religious youth workers, more than nine in ten congregations say they have a problem with keeping high school students involved in church — compared to 9 percent who say they are doing a good job reaching out to youth.[3] Inconsistency, irrelevance, independence, lack of other people their age, and school pressure are just a few reasons why kids turn away from church.[4]

One reason teens and church may not mix well is because teens go unprepared. Most people have never been taught how to get something out of church. Another reason teens may resist church is because they aren't debriefed afterward. In other words, do we discuss at the table, "What went on at church? What did you think of the sermon? What are your questions?" [5]

I've mentioned it elsewhere in this book, and I'll say it again. This is a spiritual survival time! This is a matter of spiritual life or death for your young person. Do not play around and think, "Well, I like it, so they should like it too. It's good enough for me, so it's good enough for them." You can get fed through tapes, books, and seminars, but you have to go on a quest to find a place that has some real fire in their youth ministry — a place that will provide your young person with the greatest chance of catching the fire of God. Ask the Holy Spirit to lead you to the church you are supposed to belong to. Be open to His direction. Do not let your predisposition cloud your ability to see the truth.

Other church members will want you to stay around to rescue a dead church or to rescue a youth ministry. You start to leave and someone will make you feel guilty. "Well, your kid is the only one who sort of loves God around here and if they leave, what about all the rest?" Forget all that. You are not there to save everyone else's kids. You are there to find spiritual survival for your own. Go back to the church after they graduate from high school if you want, but right now get them in a place where they can grow — a spiritual incubator.

CHAPTER FOURTEEN . . . **WHAT TO DO IF YOUR TEENAGER THINKS THE BIBLE OR CHURCH IS BORING**

Do not take chances with your young person. They will only be young once. Do whatever it takes to get them in an environment that causes them to love going to church, love going to youth group, and love spending time in God's Word.

Jay Kesler says, "An enterprising, middle-aged businessman has moved 23 times in their 35 years of marriage and yet has one of the most successful families going. When asked how he managed this, he responded with a real pearl of wisdom. 'Every time we moved to a new town,' he said, 'the first thing we did was look for a church with a program for kids the ages of ours. Then we found a house near it. We've been Methodists, Presbyterians, Episcopalians, Baptists, Assembly of God, and Free Churchmen. We've always felt that the key to helping our mobile family was to choose the church first, then the house.'"[6]

Once you find a place where your teen loves to go, do not use it as punishment. Do not prohibit them from going if they do something wrong. There are plenty of other things you can take away from them, but don't take away any kind of spiritual activity. You will be sending the wrong message to them if you do. You think you are accomplishing the desired results because you are taking something away that they really love. But do not take away anything that encourages their love for God or anything associated with their love for God and use that against them as a punishment.

15

What to do to keep your teen on fire for the Lord

Your teen has just come back from a camp, a conference, or an "Acquire the Fire" youth convention, and they can't stop talking about what God did in their life. They just came back from a mission trip and the fire, fervor, and zeal for God has consumed their life. You have never seen anything like it! Now you just pray and hope that it stays.

What can you do to help? Maybe you are thinking, "I wonder how long it will last this time. I saw them get fired up like this before, but it died out after a few weeks." Most parents, not feeling very gifted as "youth ministers," get discouraged thinking they really cannot do anything to help keep their young person's fire burning. This is simply not true.

In a recent survey, 93 percent of the young people interviewed said they believe God loves them; 2 percent said they don't believe it; 2 percent said they don't believe in God; and 3 percent were unsure. Eighty-six percent believed that Jesus Christ was God or the Son of God; 6 percent believed that Jesus was just another religious leader; 3 percent believed that Jesus never actually lived; and 5 percent were not sure.[1]

Eighty percent of born-again Christians agree with the statement, "the Bible teaches that God helps those who help themselves," 49 percent of Christians agree "the devil, or Satan, is not a living being but is a symbol of evil," and 39 percent of born-again Christians believe "if a person is generally good, or does enough good things for others during their life, they will earn a place in heaven."[2] No wonder many young people have trouble maintaining their fire — they have been presented with an unclear picture of true Christianity!

Listen to what some teens have said:

> "I find it difficult to stay on fire for the Lord. I go to a pretty big church, but the youth group doesn't do anything."

> "It is hard to stay on fire when my parents say one thing, then do another. Their actions don't follow their words."

> "Many Christians I know are self-righteous and they are always right. I am losing interest in Christianity because most Christians I've met show more hatred than love."

> "I need more encouragement, discipline, and accountability from my parents — particularly from my dad."

> "I always feel like I'm doing something wrong in my walk with God. I wish my parents would encourage me more."

> "I'm on a roller coaster ride with God. I can't keep focused. I have tried to, but when nothing happened, I kinda gave up for a while."

CHAPTER FIFTEEN . . . WHAT TO DO TO KEEP YOUR TEEN ON FIRE FOR THE LORD

"I wish my parents would encourage me instead of nagging me. I wish they wouldn't try to make me worship their way."

What can you do? Embrace your teen's excitement. Many parents patronize their young person. "Yeah, yeah, yeah. I remember when I was that fired up." They act as if their teen is excited over a new club or a new activity. They think it's simply another passing teenage fad. Instead of patronizing your young person and playing down their newfound passion and love for Christ, embrace them and their fire.

Ask some questions about what God did in their life. What specific things can you pray for? What are they going to do differently to make sure their fire does not die? What can you as a parent do to help them maintain their fire? They may have some good suggestions for you. Ask them what decisions they made during the camp or conference that they want to be held accountable to. Ask them what makes it different this time compared to any other time before.

Don't sound like the CIA when you are asking these things, but come across as a loving, concerned parent/friend who wants to be involved in your teen's life, embracing them, and genuinely believing God has changed their life. Do not look at them all glossy-eyed and respond with a simple, "Oh, that's great, son." Really tune in to what was great about it and how their life has changed. This is the first step towards keeping it a lasting fervor for the Lord.

> **Never be lacking in zeal, but keep your spiritual fervor, serving the Lord.**
>
> Romans 12:11

Keep *your* fire burning for God. Simply stated, do not keep a spiritual "air" about you without being truly spiritual. If there are areas of your walk with the Lord that are shallow or empty, deal with them. If you need to ask for someone's forgiveness and repent — then do it! Sometimes when we see our young person get on fire, we get a little intimidated by it. We think, "What can they teach me that I haven't already learned?" and we become guilty of the very thing they have been guilty of — sitting in the back of the church, acting like we've heard it all before.

A wise person can learn from anyone. We need to realize we can learn from our teen. Instead of letting their fervor and passion for God intimidate you and cause you to act like you are more spiritual, let it inspire you to seek God like never before. Find some time to spend on your knees before the Lord. Let it push you to deeper levels of humility, deeper levels of intimacy with God, and more passionate times in reading and meditating on His Word. You'll enter new realms of fasting, praying, and staying on your knees until you hear the voice of God.

When you have a genuine fire burning passionately for God, your teen cannot help but be affected. When your relationship with God becomes stale, ritualistic, and formalized your young person's heart will grow hard. When we say things like, "I remember when I used to pray that much or read the Bible that much," we play down what our teen has by implying that it will not last very long, or that we used to have it and are now simply pretending.

Start having honest discussions with your teen regarding your Christian life and their Christian life. Do not try to be pseudo-spiritual, which your teen will interpret as fake, but seek God with more fervor than you ever have. If your young person is going after the Lord with all they've got, you have to go after Him even harder to provide true spiritual leadership for them. As you share with them your prayer concerns, your struggles, and your victories in your walk with the Lord, your young person will do the same with you. You will be on the road to a discipling relationship with your young person. But do not assume that now that they are on fire for God, they will stay that way forever. That fire must continually be fanned and encouraged in order for it to be kept burning.

In the process of establishing this type of dialogue, let there be some mutual accountability. Ask your teen to hold you accountable to having quiet times or to dealing with certain areas of your life; not so they can throw it in your face later, but so you can show a little trust and respect. Then ask them, "What can I pray for you about? What are some areas you are being challenged in that you want God to help you get through?"

When most people who get the fire of God in their life start losing it, they don't want anyone to know, so they cover up the darkness. But when the light comes in, it reveals the darkness for what it is. If you show the darkness for what it is before it becomes a problem, the darkness has no opportunity to become a stronghold. Being accountable to one another will take the friendship-intimacy factor to a whole new level in your relationship with your young person.

A fallacy many parents buy into is thinking we need to keep our young person on that spiritual mountaintop. We want them to stay there forever and ever and hope it never goes away. First of all, you cannot just hope — you must do something to keep the fire burning. Do not presume they will accidentally stay on fire forever. Also, it is helpful to know we were not meant to stay on the mountaintop. What do I mean by that? Look at the story of Jesus on the Mount of Transfiguration. Jesus went up there to pray and to have His quiet time, not necessarily to get transfigured.

> **About eight days after Jesus said this, he took Peter, John and James with him and went up onto a mountain to pray. As he was praying, the appearance of his face changed.**
>
> **Luke 9:28,29**

When Jesus was praying on the mountaintop, the presence of God appeared. Moses and Elijah were there having a conversation with Him. The disciples got so freaked out, they said, "Lord, Lord, do You want us to build a house for the three of you so You can stay around?" This is what happens when we have one encounter with God — we want to institutionalize it. We want to remember that encounter forever and ever and hope it will never end.

CHAPTER FIFTEEN . . . **WHAT TO DO TO KEEP YOUR TEEN
ON FIRE FOR THE LORD**

> **A voice came from the cloud, saying, "This is my Son,
> whom I have chosen; listen to him."**

> **Luke 9:35**

In other words, "Quit talking, man! Check out what is going
on."

In visiting the Mount of Transfiguration years ago, I discovered
that since then Christians *have* gone up there and built a church
for Jesus with two rooms — one for Elijah and one for Moses.
It is not surprising, since we've been doing that same thing in
Christianity for years. We have built whole churches and entire
denominations on one experience with God.

There is not supposed to be just one mountaintop. We are supposed to go back again and again into the presence of God. We
are not supposed to hope our young person stays on that mountain, but that they get taken to the next mountain.

What's the next challenge in their life? What's the next area
God wants them to grow in? Maybe it's going on a mission trip.
Maybe it's doing ministry in the inner city. Maybe there are
areas of their character God wants to refine. Ask the question,
"Why did God give you that fire and what is the next mountain
God wants you to climb?"

Help your teen find what that next mountain is. Help them
define the next step in their spiritual journey. They need to feel
there is someone helping and guiding them. You cannot just
depend on your pastor and youth pastor. Be the spiritual leader
of your home! Help your young person see that they have the

fire for a reason. God wants to do something in them and through them.

When they see there is another mountain to climb, they'll throw their passion and fervor into climbing that next mountain, not into just trying to keep the fire they have. In going up that next mountain, their fire will build and become stable and strong.

If you're thinking, "That's great. But I wish my kids would get some fire so I could help them keep it," take a look at the previous chapter.

16

What to do if your teen wants to go on a mission trip

There you are, trying to raise a young person who is responsible, doing all the right things with their life, going on to be a pillar in the community, and all of a sudden they come home saying they want to go on a missions trip. They want to spend the summer in another nation where the people do not speak English, and *you* have never left the country yourself!

Perhaps your young person is asking your permission to go to another country, maybe one that you have never heard of. They saw a video or got excited at a conference, and now it's all they can talk about. As parents, we tend to think it will blow over — it will pass. "They have been excited about other things, too. I will just wait for it to die down."

What's a parent to do?

It's not as strange as you might think for your young person to want to do something like this. In fact, thousands of young people every year are going on mission trips all around the world because God has touched their heart and given them a desire to go. It would be wise for us not to dismiss it as another teenage-hype experience, but to find out what we might do to encourage them to go.

God has laid missions on the hearts of young people all across the nation. Listen to what some teens have said:

> "I said that I wanted to go on a mission trip two years ago. My parents told me they would pray about it and give me an answer — they never did; so I didn't go. Then I went to an 'Acquire the Fire' and God laid it on my heart to go to Bolivia. I told my parents my decision and for some reason, they are now holding a grudge against me. I am 17 years old and really have the desire to go on missions. I know that it is God's will, but what do I do about my parents?"

> "I would just like some encouragement from my parents about going on a mission trip."

> "I want to go on a mission trip, but my parents say that I need to get a summer job and earn money for next year."

Go! I am sending you out like lambs among wolves.

Luke 10:3

Jesus sent His disciples out on short-term trips. You ask, "Why go for just two weeks or just one or two months? What good is that going to do?" Jesus sent His disciples out on short-term trips, sometimes for a week, sometimes for a couple of weeks. Someone who goes on a short-term trip can be an asset in ways that people who do long-term missions work may not be. If Jesus sent His disciples on short-term trips, surely He would know whether it is a valuable and credible way for a young person to spend their energy.

CHAPTER SIXTEEN . . . WHAT TO DO IF YOUR TEEN WANTS TO GO ON A MISSION TRIP

Sometimes we think, "Why do they need to go while they are young? Why don't they wait until they are a little bit older?" Jesus called His own disciples *lambs*. They were not even sheep yet, they were lambs. They were young. They were wet behind the ears. They did not know how to do very much. They were not very talented, and they asked a lot of stupid questions.

Maybe you feel your young person is a little too immature or not very strong in the Lord. Maybe they haven't been a Christian very long. It is exactly that youthful zeal that Jesus wants to harness and use to change the world. The fact is, an experience on the mission field during the teenage years could dramatically affect the way your teen spends the rest of their life. They can see God's hand directly involved in their life, using them to minister to people who have never heard about Jesus.

I know it is not easy to let go. While at a church where I was ministering, a man came up and grabbed my arm as I was sitting in the congregation getting ready to preach. He said, "Ron Luce, you came here a year ago and started talking about taking kids to Russia. I thought you were crazy. My daughter came home from church that day saying she wanted to go to Russia. I thought she was crazy. I told her I'd let her go if God would give her the money. God gave her the money and I thought He was crazy. So last summer I let my little girl go to Russia. It was hard being away from her for two months and I really had to use my faith to entrust her into God's hands. I got a couple postcards and a couple phone calls from her, but I was so excited to see her when she came home. I picked her up at the airport and as she was telling me all the stories of how God had used her, I thought 'Yeah, yeah, I'm just glad my baby is home.' Then when we got to the house, we put in the video tape that showed my little girl involved in ministry."

This man began to cry, and with tears streaming down his face he said, "And when I saw my baby, my own flesh and blood, passing out tracts to those people who had never heard about Christ, I knew it was worth it. I knew it was worth entrusting her into the Lord's hands and it was worth all of the finances she had raised. I realized I had made a difference by sending my little girl."

If your young person even has a little bit of an inkling to go, let them go while it is on their heart. You do not know if the desire will always be there. Seize the moment. The older they get, the more distractions there are — cars, clothes, jobs, and relationships. If your teen has that desire to go when they are young, let them go and God will do something in their heart that you could never do.

Every summer, we at Teen Mania Ministries take thousands of teenagers on mission trips with us all around the world. We have seen literally hundreds of thousands of people won to the Lord as a result of young people reaching out with their faith. I have had countless parents tell me things like, "Thank you so much for doing in my young person what I could not do as a parent. I did everything I knew to do, but having them go on this mission trip completed everything!"

Do not be like that one parent who prayed, "Oh Lord, please do not let my young person go on a mission trip. I want them to be a success in life." The Lord wants to use them in a mighty way. Send them out to the mission field while they are young — it keeps them from getting into trouble in the summer, and it will plant in their heart a vision for God to use them for the rest of their life.

If your church or denomination does not have a mission trip available, please write or call us. We will give you information on how your young person can go with us this summer or at Christmas on an adventure that will stir up their vision and change their life!

17

What to do if you find out your teen uses drugs

Your response to finding out that your teen uses drugs is similar to finding out that your teen drinks. Take a deep breath and relax before you say or do anything!

In a world that glamorizes drug use, it is easy to see why kids are drawn to using them. Between television, movies, and kids at school, our kids are bombarded with the fantasy drugs seem to offer. Drug use is rising among teenagers. The University of Michigan surveyed 50,000 students across the country and found that one in four teens uses some type of drug before high school. The study's director believes that the increase is largely due to the entertainment industry's glamorization of drugs.[1]

The number of teens smoking pot doubled between 1992 and 1994. Teens are also starting earlier. In 1991, the average first-time user was 14 to 17 years old. In 1992, that dropped to between 13 and 15.[2] One out of every ten high school seniors uses marijuana on a daily basis. Almost one in six high school seniors has tried cocaine or crack. Nearly one out of 20 sixth- to twelfth-graders have used cocaine sometime in the past year. Every day in America, 500 adolescents begin using drugs. Thirty-nine percent of fourth-graders say that "using drugs is a big problem among kids our age."[3]

Why do kids think their peers use drugs?

Reason	Age 12	Age 17
To be cool	49 percent	11 percent
Friends doing it	24 percent	25 percent
To feel good	9 percent	23 percent
Drug abuse in family	7 percent	4 percent
Stress relief	6 percent	22 percent
Personal problems	3 percent	7 percent
To rebel	1 percent	6 percent[4]

Some causes of drug use and abuse are: peer pressure, sexual or physical abuse, latchkey kids, parental example, and the need to escape. Some of the physical ramifications of drug use include leukemia, heart attack, infertility, tissue damage, and malnutrition.[5]

"I only smoked [pot] for a few months. Now I'm on drugs for the rest of my life. I thought marijuana was no big deal," says Kevin West, 19. He shot himself playing Russian roulette while high on pot, and is now paralyzed on his left side and must take anti-seizure medications daily.[6]

So what are you going to do if you find your teen in this situation? In a similar way to an alcohol discovery, I suggest the following steps:

1. Make sure you let them know you still love them, even though you do not like their behavior. Distinguish between their behavior and them as a person.

2. Think through the disciplines you want to use. As a teenager, your child is really too old for you to spank. It is time to respect them and retain their dignity as a human being. There certainly are ways that you can discipline them and make them feel the "pain," such as not letting them see their favorite movies or television shows, taking items out of their room for a certain period of time, not allowing them to have the food they want, and restricting phone calls and activities. Do not respond out of anger! Your goal is not to feel better for making them miserable about what they have done. Your goal is to make them feel the pain for what they have done so they will want to change in that area.

3. Develop a dialogue about the drug issue. Do not just tell them, "Never do it again!" and the next time you talk about it is the next time you catch them doing it. Discuss the drug issue in a number of different ways:

- Use statistics. Let them know the physical consequences from a medical standpoint.

- Use stories about young people whose lives have been really messed up as a result of drugs.

- Teach your teen why it is wrong. As in alcohol abuse, they are giving the control of their brain over to a drug. The drug dictates what they do and what they say. They are choosing to be irresponsible and flush their life down the toilet by letting drugs control them.

SUBSTANCE ABUSE

The real danger here is more than just physical, that death or an accident might occur when they are high. I'm talking about *spiritual danger.* In the Old Testament the word for "sorcery" is *pharmakeia.* Sorcery involved talking with demons and evil spirits. *Pharmakeia* is where we get our word "pharmacy." It was directly related to drug abuse. Sorcerers would smell incense, as they still do today in many tribes, and it would distort their brain. As a result, sorcery and interaction with demons was possible.

Teach your young person that as they relinquish control of their mind to a drug, they no longer have the resources to stand against the world of evil spirits. So many people have become oppressed, depressed, or possessed by an evil spirit as a result of doing drugs. They can't figure out why they are depressed, angry, and irritable all the time. They have let their guard down and have been invaded by something they never asked for and were never even aware of.

This is not just a matter of saying, "Now, young man, be a good boy and don't do those drugs." This is a matter of keeping the world of evil spirits out of your child's heart, mind, and life; keeping demons out of their life; and keeping a strong resistance against the enemy.

When people start experimenting with drugs, they wonder why their lives suddenly take a totally different direction. They just invited in a whole world of evil without necessarily realizing it. People say, "I never invited the devil into my life!" But you don't have to do that verbally. If you let your guard down, the devil and his demons will gladly enter your life.

If your young person is doing drugs, it is imperative you pray over them in the name of Jesus and rebuke the devil. If your teen has not given their life to the Lord, tell them how important it is, now more than ever, to invite Jesus into their life and forgive them. Then take a stand against the enemy. Rebuke the devil in the name of Jesus. "In the name of Jesus, any evil spirit or any demon that may have tried to oppress me or possess me as a result of letting my self-control and my guard down, I rebuke you. You have no part of my life, in Jesus' name. Amen."

I encourage you to begin the process of ongoing education about drugs and why they are wrong. Help them to understand the *why* rather than just giving them a *no*. You will be amazed at how responsive your young person will be if you are telling them *why*. Give them a resource of weaponry to use when they feel peer pressure — when friends try to talk them into doing drugs. Give them an arsenal of reasons and information why not to take drugs. They will convince their friends that what they are doing is totally irrational and uncalled for. When it becomes *their* conviction, and not just *yours,* your teen will be unstoppable.

SUBSTANCE ABUSE

18

What to do if you know or think your young person is using tobacco

Cigarette smoking went from being a simple pastime to a mark of independence, rebellion, and maturity among teenagers in the '50s. Since then, each generation has experienced various phases of popularity and symbolism. Today's teenagers are no different. It's been proven that cigarette advertising is marketed towards young people, as in the case of Joe Camel, who was recently banned from advertisements.

The tobacco companies know they won't make much money from teens while they are young, but if they can get them to experiment with smoking, there is the potential of making money off them throughout their lifetimes. If tobacco companies get them while they are young, they will have them for life.

Why do young people use tobacco? They are trying to communicate:

"I belong."

"I am grown up."

"I am tough."

"I am angry."

The final reason young people smoke is that it is truly an addiction.[1] Eighty-five percent of all smokers wish they could quit. One young person said, "I've tried to quit smoking; but it just doesn't work. No matter how hard I try or pray, I always fall back."

Thirty-five percent of all high school students smoke cigarettes. This represents a greater percentage than that of adult smokers — 25 percent. The figure for teens rose 7 percent since 1991, and the figure for adults has dropped 20 percent since the '70s. About 84 percent of children think cigarette advertising promotes at least one benefit from smoking. Among 16- to 17-year-olds, 76.2 percent said cigarette ads depict the habit as enjoyable; 73 percent view it as relaxing; 67 percent saw smoking as a means of reducing stress; and 41 percent believe advertisements depict smoking as a way of staying thin.[2]

Chewing tobacco is also on the rise. The harmful effects of chewing tobacco are becoming more and more blatant and obvious.

What should you do if you suspect your teenager is one of those who uses tobacco, either once in a while or all the time? Have you found some cigarette butts in their room? Have you smelled smoke on their breath or clothes? They seem to have all the right excuses for smelling smoky when they come in at night. "I was in a restaurant in the smoking section."

You're thinking, "Well, at least I don't smell alcohol on their breath...or at least she's not pregnant. If smoking is all my young person is doing, then I can be thankful for that." Can you really? How do you know that is the only thing they are doing?

How should you approach the subject with your young person? Here are some suggestions:

The first thing you should be concerned about is not necessarily the act of smoking, which ultimately can be very harmful physically, but your relationship with your teen. The goal is not to catch them red-handed or prove beyond a shadow of a doubt they are smoking just so you can get in their face. The goal is to have an incredibly great relationship with your young person so you can continue teaching them how to live a responsible life.

If they are smoking, or if you suspect they are smoking, then you have a larger problem than just their smoking. If they aren't telling you anything about it and are coming up with too many excuses as to why their breath or clothes are smoky, the problem is not simply the use of tobacco, it is your relationship with them.

Why do they feel like they need to sneak around? How is it you are so distant from them that they cannot be honest and upfront with you? If you just suspect they are smoking or using tobacco, the most important issue at this point is not to get to the bottom of whether they are or not. The issue is to dive into a heart-to-heart relationship with them, loving them, being concerned about their life — what they are going through, what they are thinking, and what they are feeling.

If you have that best-friend relationship with them, the ideal situation is that they would come running to you if they are even tempted with a cigarette, not to mention if they had actually tried one. So if they have not told you, you need to

SUBSTANCE ABUSE

work on improving your relationship — not just proving or disproving the fact that they are or are not smoking.

The next major issue concerning smoking is the people with whom your young person is hanging around — those who are most likely luring them into it. Most young people don't start smoking because one day that idea pops into their minds. Whether on purpose or by accident, they have surrounded themselves with people who are attracted to smoking, for whatever reason. The subculture of being macho or grown-up has brainwashed them into thinking this is the thing they ought to do.

Something about having a cigarette in their hands, blowing smoke out their mouths, and hanging around others who do the same brings a sense of camaraderie and belonging. It means your young person has grown closer to this group of young people who smoke than they have to you. They find it is more important for them to be associated with this group than with you as their parent and family.

How well do you know their friends? Do you know who they hang out with at school? Do you know who they associate with after school? At this age friendships are extremely important. Young people place an incredible amount of value on their peers' opinion of them. It can be desperately important for them to belong to a certain group because their identities are wrapped up in their friends.

If this is the case, no amount of lecturing about how bad smoking is and no amount of punishment for smoking will do much good. The power of peer pressure is considerably more influential, because they desperately want to belong. And "belonging" to that group by smoking could be the beginning of worse things to come.

It starts with smoking, then it can progress to wild parties and drug use. The road to destruction can be a difficult one to get off. Of course your teen will not agree. They will say, "Sure. I'm smoking a cigarette and the next thing you know I'm a drug addict! I don't think so!" It won't make any sense to them, and they will think you are overreacting.

What do you do? You begin to investigate who your young person's peers are — who they hang out with, who they are naturally drawn to, and who they spend their free time with. Get to know these people. Invite them over to the house. Find out what makes them tick. See if they are the type of people you really want rubbing off on your young person.

If not, it may be time to take drastic measures. It may be time for you to move to a different part of the city or to a different state. It may be time for you to find another church if the young people at church smoke. (If you think none of the young people in the youth group smoke, don't kid yourself!) It might mean enrolling them in another school.

Do what it takes to salvage the teenage years of your child while they are still salvageable. However, just making these changes is not the solution. Unless they have a change of heart, your young person will find the same type of people with the same attitudes wherever they go.

You will have to take overt steps to get them in the right peer group. That may mean finding a fired-up youth group, sending them on a mission trip, or getting them to a youth conference

SUBSTANCE ABUSE

or camp. Get them in a fired-up environment and keep them there until they catch what's there.

Notice they didn't start smoking the first day they went to a new school. They had to spend time with those people and get familiar with them before they started smoking or having the bad attitude. The same applies to catching the fire of God — the fire of wanting to do what is right, holy, true, and truthful. You have to help them become comfortable there until they begin to make some real friends.

You can show them pictures of people with lung cancer and of people who have chewed tobacco for 20 years. It might serve as enough shock value to wake them up and make them realize that smoking is not all the "fun" it's cracked up to be.

Show your young person scriptures like 1 Corinthians 6:19, which says, **Your body is a temple of the Holy Spirit.** If they have given their life to Jesus, God lives inside their body. *He lives in them.* They need to treat their body like a temple. God created their body to function a certain way, and the more they cram stuff in it like tobacco, the more they are destroying the very thing God gave them to live in. Hopefully this will serve as some motivation to those genuinely interested in the things of God and in wanting to serve Him.

Above all, do not pass off smoking as a phase they are going through. "It will pass. It's not that big of a deal." In too many cases, smoking is the first step toward a much bigger deal. Their present relationship with you and the friends they surround themselves with is an indication they are going down the wrong path. Take action now!

19

What to do if your teen is drinking or going to parties

You have discovered, maybe through an anonymous tip or their bloodshot eyes and irrational behavior, that your young person has been drinking alcohol. It started by going to a few parties with their friends. You thought they would never drink — so did they. It may be just a few beers, it may be getting drunk once in a while, or it may be a real drinking problem.

Seventy-nine percent of students say it is easy to get alcohol. Seventy-seven percent say alcohol is common at parties. Forty-one percent say some of their friends have a problem with alcohol, and 22 percent have ridden in a car with someone who has been drinking.[1]

Before you fly off the handle and destroy the possibility of a relationship with your young person, take a deep breath. Realize they are still the same person on the inside as they were before they began drinking. They are still your child. And they will remember the way you respond to this intense crisis for the rest of their life.

What exactly should you do? Most importantly, think through how to approach the situation and really talk about it with your young person. You don't want to come off as a parent who just says, "Don't do it again," and that's all you have to say. There is more going on in their life and their mind that has pushed them to this level.

Ask yourself this question, "How much have I really taught them about drinking — the physical dangers and the emotional effects?" It is easy for parents simply to tell their young person not to drink; but it is another thing to teach them why they shouldn't based upon principles rather than just because you said so.

While expressing the fact that, although you do not approve of or like their behavior, you still love and appreciate them, it is important they understand both are very true. Just because you do not like their behavior does not mean you do not like them. It seems like a small distinction to us, but it is huge to a young person. Jesus did things like that all the time, as with the woman who was caught in adultery. He did not condemn her or put her down, but at the same time, He was very clear. He told her, "Go and sin no more." (See John 8:11.)

Think about the disciplinary measures you need to implement. Don't just say, "Don't do that again." If they are going against your wishes in doing this, there ought to be a price to pay — working around the house, giving up privileges, restricting phone calls, etc. Tell them drinking is wrong and you do not want them doing it, but back that up with consequences that will make them think. Do not discipline out of anger! But think about what will make your young person feel the sting of having gone against your wishes.

Educate your teen by sharing the following:

According to research, in 1993 an average of 14,000 Americans *per hour* got behind the wheel after drinking too much. Alcohol-related crash deaths totaled more than 17,000 in 1995. One of every 12 instances involved an underage drinker.[2]

Find some local stories of young people who were driving drunk and have gone to jail or were involved in a tragic car accident.

The Bible says in Proverbs 20:1, **Wine is a mocker and beer a brawler; whoever is led astray by them is not wise.** The Bible plainly tells us that if you drink, you are going to be mocked. You are going to do stupid things — things that you may not remember and will likely regret.

God designed you to be in charge of your mind and in charge of your life. In Genesis 1:26 God says He gives us **rule over the fish of the sea and the birds of the air, over the livestock, over all the earth, and over all the creatures that move along the ground.** He gave us dominion. He put us in charge of the world.

When you choose to drink, you give charge of your brain over to a drug. A drug is now in charge of you. Alcohol is now in charge of your brain. You are not taking responsibility for your life. You begin the process of slowly flushing your life down the toilet.

Wine is a mocker. Ultimately, the very alcohol you drink will end up mocking you and laughing in your face because it destroyed your life. You become a slave to it. Romans 6:16 says, **Don't you know that when you offer yourselves to someone to obey him as slaves, you are slaves** to the one whom you obey — whether you are slaves to sin, which leads to death, or to obedience, which leads to righteousness?

If you choose to obey and submit yourself to alcohol, you are no longer a slave to the Lord. You are no longer the master of your own destiny. You have become the slave of a fermented grape. Drinking may seem like the tough, cool thing to do, but ultimately you degenerate as a human being.

Discuss object lessons as you drive by bars or when you see alcohol in stores. Say things like, "There are people in there right now who are hurting and broken, not knowing that the real answer is to give their lives to God. There are people in there who could have been doctors, lawyers, authors, or inventors, but they flushed their potential down the toilet of alcohol."

Develop this process of teaching, training, and constantly expounding on the craziness and foolishness of using alcohol, and it will help your teen develop their own conviction. They will get to where they are no longer refraining from it only because you asked them to, but because they see it will wreck their life.

20

What to do if your teen has no real Christian friends

If the people your teen hangs out with are generally not saved, or are saved but not walking with the Lord, this should be a cause of great concern to you. Who is your young person naturally attracted to or most readily drawn to? Who do they enjoy spending most of their time with?

Most young people have two sets of friends — their *church* friends and their *real* friends at school. Most of the time they don't want to be seen with their church friends when they are around their school friends. Most of the time their church friends are not really friends at all, they are acquaintances. They hang around them every week because their parents drag them to church, but they are not people they would choose to be around.

Parents pass it off with, "Well, these other kids may not be radical Christians, but they are *good kids*." The problem is, a lot of *good kids* get into a lot of big trouble. The power of friendships and peer pressure among teenagers is something most parents don't remember and cannot identify with. We hear about peer pressure, but we don't understand much of the tangled web of relationships it weaves.

Peer pressure is not reserved only for teenagers. We can see the effects of peer pressure among adults. Someone gets a nice car, so the neighbor has to get a nicer one. How many are always wanting a better job, more pay, a bigger house, a bigger ring, or nicer clothes? Although it is obvious, we tend not to mention it or notice it as much among adults, but we make it a huge issue among teenagers.

You will hear me talk a number of times about peer pressure in several of these chapters, because it is such a huge influence on young people's lives.

Researchers have found that teenagers pick friends with a similar age, sex, sexual experience, and academic and cultural orientation. Most teenagers place great importance on their friendships. About 62 percent of high school seniors surveyed say it's extremely important to have strong friendships. Teenagers spend more time with their friends each day than they do with their father, mother, both parents, or other adults — four hours with friends as compared to one hour with both parents.

Nine out of ten teenagers say they experience peer pressure, and fewer than half of them say they try to stop peer pressure. The *TeenAge Magazine* reader survey also found that 80 percent of young people give in to peer pressure at least once a week, and 60 percent admit they pressure others.[1]

As you can see from these statistics, the opinions young people listen to most are those of their peers. So the question is, what peers does your young person choose to be around? Many parents feel totally helpless, as though they have no influence over their teenager's friends. This is simply not the truth.

You think, "Well, I have no control over who they meet at school." On the contrary, you *do* have control over where they go to school, what kind of school they go to, what extracurricular activities they do and with whom, and most importantly, what church and youth group they attend.

He who walks with the wise grows wise, but a companion of fools suffers harm.

Proverbs 13:20

If you want your young person to be wise, get them around wise young people. If you let them hang around fools, they will end up suffering harm and their life will be the worse for it.

"Just because they are not saved, does that mean they are a fool?" Psalm 53:1 says **The fool says in his heart, "There is no God."** If they are not Christians, or are carnal Christians, ultimately they are going to do some very foolish things with their life because they have no reason not to. They have no moral strength, and they have nothing guiding them greater than themselves.

As parents we must do everything we can to influence our kids to be around wise young people. I am not talking about those who are straight-A students. I am talking about young people who are wise in how they use their free time, how they spend money, and how they develop relationships and friendships.

Church youth groups can be helpful. "Since peers exert so much influence, a group of 'good kids' could push our teens in the right direction. This is where the church youth group and other Christian youth organizations come into the picture. They

PEER PRESSURE/FRIENDSHIPS

can provide Christian friends, a wholesome atmosphere, and solid content."[2]

Charles R. Swindoll shares a story about his children:

> "We tried to get them to think about the type of people they wanted to spend their time with — people who would strengthen them morally, people with good self-esteem. We stressed the advantage of finding friends with good parents and homes with high ideals. I remember when one of our daughters chose a friend who wasn't good for her. She's a sensitive girl and was easily swayed in her early years. We sat her down one day and just talked about her friend — what her home life was like, and what the characteristics of her family seemed to be. Then we asked our daughter what things she liked in our home and what was important to her.
>
> "I asked her to think about the parallels between her life and the life she wanted, and that of her new friend. As I suspected, she couldn't think of too many. By realizing that there was such a marked contrast between her life and ideals and those of her new friend, my daughter began to see things in a new light."[3]

Some key concepts to consider:

1. **Relationship.** Become a "peer" in your young person's life. I'm not suggesting you act like a teenager and try to fit into the adolescent world — that would be foolish. But it is possible to build an open, *influential* relationship by doing

things together, talking, listening, and accepting them as emerging adults.

2. **Dialogue.** If you want to steer your kids toward the right kind of friends, you must open channels of communication. Show genuine interest in them and their activities and spend time just talking things over.

3. **Open home.** Let your kids know your home is open for their friends. Instead of condemning their peers and pointing out their faults, invite them to dinner or some other social opportunity.

You are going to hear comments from your young person like, "All the Christians I meet are weird. I can trust my non-Christian friends more than I can my Christian friends." And that is probably true. Adults could say the same thing. Yet in spite of all that, there *are* young people who passionately love God with all their hearts. Those are the ones you need to find a way to get your teen around. The question is *how.*

First of all, diligently search until you find an incredible youth group or youth ministry for your young person to be a part of on a regular basis. Scour your city. Look in to every church that has anything going on that is really solid. I'm not talking about a bunch of fluff and hype. I'm talking about a group of kids who are going after God with all their hearts. They are fun, they are motivated, they are excited, they are cool — and they love God with all their hearts.

I know parents who have moved to a new town and taken another job in order to go to a church with a fired-up youth group. Do not choose a church simply based on whether *you*

PEER PRESSURE/FRIENDSHIPS

like the Sunday morning service or not. This is a matter of life or death for them because of the fact that peers are such an incredibly strong influence in teenagers' lives.

Secondly, take your young person to every kind of Christian youth activity you can find. Some parents find something their child really likes and then begin to use that as a punishment if they do something wrong. "You can't go to youth group tonight because you did that," or "You can't go to that Christian concert," or "You can't go to this camp because you did such and such."

Little do parents realize that they are cutting off the *spiritual growth* of their young person as a penalty for what they have done wrong. There are plenty of other things you can use as a means of correction without having to take them away from the things of God.

I know it is a sacrifice to run them back and forth to church and to different activities, but we do it for the sake of sports, ballet, cheerleading, etc., and all those things will pass away. We will barely remember the scores on the scoreboard — but how they walk with God will direct the rest of their lives.

Getting your teen around a group of young people long enough to really develop friendships means letting them go on retreats, to camp, to conventions, and on mission trips. It will help their walk with God. It will help them gain real friends who really love God.

When your young person finds some real friends who are going after the Lord with all their hearts, 90 percent of the problems with your young person will be solved. They will be hanging around wise people and, therefore, they will be getting wiser. Because peers are such a great influence, they will be constantly influencing each other to seek more of God.

Do not settle for the fact you have always gone to that church, the youth group is good enough, and Pastor Joe is an okay youth pastor. For the sake of your young person, their walk with God, and their survival as a Christian, do whatever is necessary to make sure they are constantly around young people who really have the fire of God.

You might say, "Well, they have to stand strong in a secular school, so shouldn't they learn how to mix well with unsaved people?" Most of their life they are going to be around unsaved people. Right now is the time, in the formulating stages of your teen's life, for them to stay around as many on-fire young people as they possibly can. Your teen will be a teenager only once.

PEER PRESSURE/FRIENDSHIPS

21

What to do if your young person wants to go out on a date

Have you noticed a little glow in your teen's eye that has never been there before? Does it seem to be getting brighter every time you see them? You don't know what could possibly be going on for them to be so full of energy and life these past few weeks. You're thinking it was your awesome job at parenting lately that has caused this sudden turn of events. They have finally realized what an incredible set of parents they have and how great it is to be part of this family.

Your young person asks if they can sit down and talk to you for a little while because they have something important to say. You're thinking it will be one of those moments that they embellish you with the compliments every parent desires to hear. Then out of nowhere, your teen begins to tell you about this girl who has been noticing them lately and now they have the courage to ask her out on a date. Never mind the fact that they are only 14 years old. Never mind the fact that you have been the one nurturing them since they were brought into this world, providing food, shelter, and pizza at their beck and call. Suddenly, someone else has captured their heart, has grabbed their attention, and you are doomed to be the one who is to judge whether or not this possible relationship can go forward or not.

What is a parent to do?

Some parents think they have no choice — their teen will pursue a romantic relationship anyway, so why fight it. They feel like they have to say yes, and as a result, open the door to a whole new set of arguments, frustrations, and confusions. They assume this is just a normal stage in the development of a teenager's life. The issue is not whether you say yes or no about your teen going on this date. The issue is bigger than that.

What have you taught your young person about dating before this point? "What is there to teach? Don't they learn enough from school and television?" Watch out! Your teen has learned it from the wrong place! Have they learned it from those who are least qualified to teach the right way to pursue godly love, dating, or a relationship? Have you taught them to *pray* about dating someone? The cute girl or the cool guy your teen is interested in may be sending all the right signals, but unless you and your teen have a peace from God, the relationship should go no further than a friendship.

Society has bombarded our teens with what looks like the fun or popular way to pursue a dating relationship. You don't have to look very far to see the results of those types of relationships: broken hearts, immorality, and broken marriages. It is imperative that we teach our young people about relationships in general. This includes learning how to develop friendships which can ultimately lead to a happy romance.

Your child's wanting to go on a date may be just the motivation needed to start a series of conversations that can help you teach them how a godly relationship should develop. Instead of just saying yes or no right off the bat, you may want to begin by saying, "You know I was wanting to talk to you about relationships anyway, and about some of the wise principles in developing the right kind of relationship. Let's talk about this." Let me share with you some of those principles and diffuse some of the commonly held myths about teenage dating.

Myth #1: If I don't date, I won't be popular — I won't have any fun as a teenager and everyone will see me as totally weird.

Young people are raised with the notion that they must date. It is not a matter of *if*, it is a matter of *when* and *who*. There is no wisdom or forethought put into what kind of person they should go out with or how to properly begin a relationship.

The fact is, there are thousands of young people who have fun every night of the week and don't have a boyfriend or girlfriend. They have a set of wholesome friends who know how to laugh heartily, get wild, and be crazy without their hearts being attached to another person. In the long run, they will have much more fun with a group of friends than they would by being a part of the dating scene.

Myth #2: Falling in love is just a normal part of growing up. Everyone is bound to do it and get their heart broken.

Statistics say the average person falls in and out of love ten times before they marry. Think about that. What does that say? The average person falls in love, breaks up, gets their heart ripped out — No. 1. They fall in love again, break up, get their heart ripped out — No. 2. They fall in love again and again

PEER PRESSURE/FRIENDSHIPS

until No. 10. Their heart is literally broken ten different times before they finally find the one they are going to marry. Then they walk down the aisle, look at one another gleefully in the eye, and say, "Here is the one little leftover piece of my heart I saved for you."

I don't believe that is God's best or His plan for marriage! Song of Songs 2:7 says, **Do not arouse or awaken love until it so desires.** That is repeated two more times in Song of Songs 3:5 and 8:4. What does it mean? It is making reference to physical sex and the act of "making love," but it also indicates opening the heart and allowing it to be ripped apart.

There is a part of a young person's heart and life that is not safe to open up to anyone until they are ready to develop a relationship that will last the rest of their life. The problem is that most young people cannot distinguish which part of their heart is which. Proverbs 4:23 says, **Above all else, guard your heart, for it is the wellspring of life.** We need to teach our young people to guard their hearts.

Just because they see "falling in love" as a routine occurrence on television or among friends does not mean it is the right thing or the healthy thing to do. Hearts are getting smashed left and right, over and over again, and people act like it's a normal part of growing up. Yes, it is a normal part in the lives of those who don't have wisdom, who don't know there is a wiser way, and who don't know enough to keep their hearts from getting busted wide open. I'm not saying not to let your teen go on a date. I am saying you need to teach them the wise way to pursue a relationship.

Most parents grew up having fallen in and out of love, and we kind of like the idea that it might be happening to our young person. "It is so sweet. It is so nice. You can see the sparkle in their eye." Then your young person loses their purity. "What did you do that for? What is wrong with you? Didn't I teach you better than that?!"

Many young people who have committed to purity end up getting involved sexually — not because they meant to, but because they gave their heart away. Many well-meaning people who gave their heart away first and then their body have lived with remorse for years after. They couldn't understand how it happened. *Giving your heart away to another person puts the other person in control of your life.* They can jerk the heart-string and make you do whatever they want you to. You end up doing things you never thought you would.

Teach your young person to hold on to their heart. They can have acquaintances and they can have fun with people, but they shouldn't let their heart go. Warn your child not to open their heart before they are mature enough to know what to do with those feelings. If you teach them early in life, it will save them years of heartache and heartbreak.

If you really teach this to your teen and help them develop a value of their own that says, "I don't want to mess up my heart. I don't want to give my heart away to someone else," they will no longer view it solely as your rule. They should give their heart to Jesus, and save the rest for the one they will spend the rest of their life with.

Help your teen understand that a healthy *romance* must first start with a healthy *friendship*. A sparkle in someone's eye

PEER PRESSURE/FRIENDSHIPS

sitting across the room in geometry class is not an ingredient of a healthy friendship. At the end of a breakup, most young people — as well as older people — will say, "I would never have dated that person if I had really known them." But regarding people they have known for a long time, they say, "Oh! I know them way too well. We are too good of friends to date." They are contradicting themselves and don't even know it!

Statistics show that most people date because they want someone to share their heart with. They want a real friend. But most dating in America is so plastic and contrived that the very thing they want — a close friendship with someone — is the very thing they don't get.

They are trying to be what they think the other person wants, and with both people doing that, no one ever really knows what the other person is really like. Once your teen asks you if they can go out on a date, begin a series of conversations that will help them understand the right way to pursue a relationship.

Teach them about courtship rather than dating. Help your teen understand they don't need to play the American dating game in which their heart gets broken so many different times before they get married. Courtship begins with a wholesome friendship when you think they are mature enough, wise enough, and strong enough to handle a romance. They should be accountable to parents, friends, and leaders so they don't accidentally slip up and give away their purity. Have them set guidelines on the kind of person they want to date, the kind of person they want to be before they date, and how they want to carry themselves in a dating relationship — *before* they enter one.

CHAPTER TWENTY-ONE . . . WHAT TO DO IF YOUR YOUNG PERSON WANTS TO GO OUT ON A DATE

You might say this is much too complicated for a young person — they just want to go on a date. Not so! I have seen dozens of young people who have committed to courtship instead of dating and have been spared the brokenheartedness of lost purity and the brokenheartedness of lost trust. They have aborted the legacy of relationship mishaps that scar so many of our pasts.

This is not a hoax, a dream, or a fairy tale. This is reality — living life by principles found in the Word of God. It will rescue your young person from so much of what you as a parent have already been through.

You can't regulate your young person's heart. You can't tell them who they love and who they don't. But you can help them sort out what real love is. This world demonstrates many different forms of infatuation and purports them all to be *love*. We must help our teens sort through the confusion.

As you teach them on an ongoing basis the principles of real friendship, of wholesome relationships, and of godly, wholesome romance, they will begin to take on their own values and develop their relationships according to wisdom. We can help keep our teens from awakening their love before it is time.

22

What to do if your teen is sexually active

If you are reading this chapter, your heart is probably sick and broken to know your little girl or young man is no longer sexually pure. The thing you dreaded happening has happened, or you have good reason to believe it may have happened. Before you get overwhelmed with, "If I had only..." thoughts, let me say that there are a lot of things we can all do to be better parents.

Remorse about your own performance as a parent will not help your young person at this point. What is important now is how you respond to the situation, that you rescue and salvage the relationship between you and your teenage son or daughter.

Listen to what some teens have said:

"I am sexually active and I feel like it is unstoppable."

"My mom knows that I am sexually active, but she doesn't do anything about it."

"All my mom did was take me to the doctor and have them talk to me about sex."

According to George Barna of the Barna Research Group, only 23 percent of the post-baby boomer generation claim to be virgins. Sexual activities among this generation is likewise disturbing. By age eighteen, 27 percent have experienced sexual intercourse and 55 percent have engaged in fondling breasts.

Why do teens have sex? Girls and guys responded differently:

61 percent of girls and 23 percent of boys cite pressure from the dating partner as a reason teens have sex.

59 percent of girls and 51 percent of boys say it happens because they think they are ready.

45 percent of girls have sex because they want to be loved, while 28 percent of boys give that reason.

38 percent of girls are afraid of being teased about their virginity, compared to 43 percent of boys.[1]

In *Josh McDowell's Handbook on Counseling Youth,* McDowell gives several reasons for premarital sex:

1. **Educational and Societal Messages.** The messages thrown at young people by society in general and by educational programs in particular are reasons for sexual activity.

2. **Low Level of Religious Commitment.** More frequent attendance at religious services leads to more restrictive attitudes concerning premarital sex and less sexual experience.

3. **Family Structure.** The effects of divorce and other family disruption and separation have been documented in numerous studies. One of those effects is sexual activity.

4. **Poor Sex Education at Home.** Kids who don't find the answers at home often learn the answers by painful experience. In the words of one teen, "Teenagers are ignorant about what they're doing. All they know is that they were made with certain body parts, so they might as well find out what they're used for. Sort of like test-driving a car just to see how well it performs."

5. **Relational Needs.** Many young people are uncertain of their parents' love. One girl wrote: "When I was eight years old, I first had sex with a boy of 15. I did it because I lacked love and attention from my parents. I need love and my parents never show me any. Nothing changed at home, and at 15 I became pregnant...[and] had an abortion. Now I'm afraid to date anyone, and I cry myself to sleep every night."

6. **Early Dating.** The younger a girl begins to date, the more likely she is to have sex before graduating from high school. It is also true of boys and girls who go steady in the ninth grade. Of girls who begin dating at twelve, 91 percent had sex before graduation — compared to 56 percent who dated at thirteen, 53 percent who dated at fourteen, 40 percent who dated at fifteen, and 20 percent who dated at sixteen.

7. **Peer Pressure.** A study of a thousand teens showed that 76 percent would go far enough sexually to feel experienced and not feel left out.

8. **Alcohol and Drugs.** The use of alcohol and other drugs hastens many kids' sexual involvement.

9. **Desire for a Child.** Although most youth want desperately to avoid becoming pregnant, some teenage girls are motivated to become sexually active by a desire to have a child. She may feel so bad about herself and so unloved that she tries intentionally to have a child, someone she can love and who will love her back.[2]

The top reason teenagers have sex, according to 61 percent of the girls, is a "boy pressuring them."[3]

When a young person reaches puberty, it's safe to assume the struggle with sexual desires has begun. You can make a number of observations to determine the intensity of your child's struggle. How does your son look at girls? Have you found pornographic magazines in your teen's possession? How does your daughter talk about boys? Does she emphasize only their looks and not their personalities? When with a member of the opposite sex, does your teen constantly need to be touching?[4]

How should you respond to your teen? First, be sure you show them you still love and care for them. Sometimes the reaction can be so intense from a parent's hurt, anger, and frustration that it pushes the young person further away until there is little hope of helping them regain their moral strength. Do not be so struck with shock that you fail to remember that inside that body is the real person. Most times the body has grown up a lot faster than the mind, will, and emotions. Right now your teen needs direction, someone who believes in them, and someone who is willing to help them gain wisdom in this situation.

The second thing you need to do is take a deep breath. Now that you have taken a deep breath and calmed down, let us backtrack a bit and ask a few difficult questions. How much have you talked to your child about sex? While 75 percent of parents have talked to teens about sex, less than half discussed birth control and only 55 percent discussed sexually transmitted diseases.

How much have you really explained to them? How many moral issues have you discussed with them? If you made it very clear to them that sex before marriage and any kind of petting before marriage is wrong, have you told them why? The world has inundated this generation with so much sexual indiscretion that it seems normal to a young person to have sex on the first date. The world promotes that it is morally okay to sleep around as long as you are not sleeping around with more than one person at a time.

With all that bombardment of the world's values, what have we done to bombard our children with the right message? Fifty-eight percent of teens say they don't have enough information on using different kinds of birth control. Seventy-five percent say they know how girls get pregnant, but lack practical information about using contraception.

It is God's will that you should be sanctified: that you should avoid sexual immorality.

1 Thessalonians 4:3

The body is not meant for sexual immorality, but for the Lord, and the Lord for the body.

1 Corinthians 6:13

Flee from sexual immorality. All other sins a man commits are outside his body, but he who sins sexually sins against his own body. Do you not know that your body is a temple of the Holy Spirit, who is in you, whom you have received from God? You are not your own; you were bought at a price. Therefore honor God with your body.

1 Corinthians 6:18–20

We must help our young person understand why premarital sex is wrong. The world thinks of a thousand creative ways of cramming their message down our child's throat. We need to be more creative than just telling them it is wrong. We need to help them understand sex from God's perspective — why He invented it and why it is the wise and righteous thing not to be involved until you are with your lifelong partner in marriage.

The goal is for your young person to thoroughly understand the issues pertaining to sex so they will have the moral strength in their own conscience to say no — not just because their parents said not to do it, but because they know it is wrong and it's going to mess them up.

For some reason your young person did not have that full understanding. *Now* it is time to impart an understanding of what is right and wrong and the *why* behind it. I have found that young people don't mind if there are intense "dos" and "don'ts" as long as they can understand *why.*

When we say, "Don't ask why — just do it because I say so...and because the Bible says so," they often rebel. They are not children anymore. They are young adults and they want some understanding of *why.* Now it is time for you to become an expert of the *why* behind abstaining from sexual activity so you can share with your teen, not like a professor lecturing a student, but as a friend helping another friend.

Something has happened within your child as a result of their sexual activity. They are still your child, but in a sense, they have grown up and experienced a part of adulthood prematurely. As you try to help them understand the *whys*, it is important not to cram it down their throat, come off as "holier than thou," or act like you are trying to rescue them.

It is fine to express your disappointment in their *activity*, but don't express disappointment in *them*. Please make that clear. In fact, I would not even use the word "disappointment." Instead say, "I do not like your actions, but I still love you as a person." Then you can do some research and discuss the following:

1. **Find health statistics.** There is a huge risk of disease. Tell them how many cases of venereal diseases are caught each year by teens. How many teens contract the AIDS virus each year. What percent of condoms do not work, which means that even if a condom is being used, the teen can still be giving someone AIDS or getting someone pregnant. Having sex with someone is like having sex with all the partners they have had sex with in the last seven years. If any of them

have a string of HIV or any other sexually transmitted disease, they can contract it — even with a condom.

Tell your young person statistics about these things to let them know you care and that you know what you are talking about. One of the very reasons it is wrong, why God does not want sex outside of marriage, is because it is so easy to contract a disease. If you have just one life partner, it is impossible to contract these diseases.

2. **Find pregnancy statistics.** How many girls get pregnant every year? How many girls have an abortion every year? Discuss the issue of messing up their life with a pregnancy. It causes them to have to make difficult decisions about keeping the baby or giving it away, and difficult decisions about stepping up to be a father to a child. Everyone says, "It couldn't happen to me," but for a million girls this year it has happened. That means a million guys had to face these things as well, most of whom are not taking responsibility for their actions.

3. The media has a tremendous influence on teens' sexual activity. Thirty-three percent of 12- to 18-year-olds say the media influenced their decision to have sex, with more than half citing that their birth-control training came from television or the movies. More than half (53 percent) of teenage girls get their sex education from television and movies, and more than one-third say fashion magazines are an important source of information about sex. One-third of all teenagers say the media encourages them to have sex. Thirty-four percent say some teens have sex because television and movies make it seem normal.[5]

CHAPTER TWENTY-TWO . . . **WHAT TO DO IF YOUR TEEN IS SEXUALLY ACTIVE**

First Corinthians 6:16 says, **Do you not know that he who unites himself with a prostitute is one with her in body?** "Is one with her" is a very strong statement. When your teen unites themselves sexually with another person, they do not become one with them spiritually, but their souls have touched. They have experienced the greatest intimacy possible between two human beings. Something happens in their mind, will, and emotions — the three parts of their soul — they get connected. They have bared themselves both physically and emotionally before another person, which makes them vulnerable. The most personal, intimate part of them that anyone could ever know, someone now knows.

Only one person should ever have the privilege of enjoying that very precious and private part of them.

Our society does not understand the value of intimacy. People are casually intimate with just about anyone, and it has lost its importance and value. Intimacy within marriage has become less valuable also. People's hearts, minds, wills, and emotions get profoundly confused and messed up when they continue to change sexual partners and fool around with anyone who comes along. They wonder why they feel empty, shallow, and hollow — unable to make commitments. It is important you have them pray this to break that soul tie. "In Jesus' name, I refuse to allow this emotional attachment to this person to confuse me and draw me away from God's best for my life."

5. Teach your young person about the preciousness of intimacy. Intimacy is not just sexual intercourse. They should not allow someone to touch any private parts of their body for any reason at any time. People say it is okay to

fool around as long as you don't have sex. It is not! The privacy of their body should be reserved for the one person who has the courage and desire to commit their whole life to them for the rest of their life — the person they marry. And only *after* the marriage ceremony. It is the gift God has given them to give to another person. They do not want anyone else to unwrap the package before it is given to the right person. They want to be able to walk down the aisle on their wedding day and look their bride- or groom-to-be in the eye and say, "I have saved myself for you. Not just my virginity, but my privacy has been reserved for you, and I give myself to you." Teach your young person the *value* and *honor* of being pure.

6. Talk to them about a second virginity. What does this mean? God cares more about the spirit of a virgin than the body of a virgin. It is possible to say, "From this point on I am going to renew my commitment to purity before God. I am going to keep a pure heart and a pure body." There are many people who have messed up physically, but you could never tell because they have such a pure heart. Then there are others who have a pure body, have never blown it physically, but their heart and mind are so polluted from the garbage of the world — from movies, magazines, and fantasies. They obey the letter of the law, but not the spirit of the law.

Restore a sense of pride and dignity in your young person. Let them know that even though they have blown it, they can walk pure from now on. Your teen can still walk down that aisle and say to their bride or groom, "I blew it when I was younger, but these past five years I have kept my heart, mind, and body pure;

and I am ready to give myself to you." There is awesome virtue in that.

There are a lot of other principles you could teach your young person about the nature of sex. Begin an open dialogue with your teen, sharing honestly about these kinds of things. Talk about what they should do if they are tempted, so as to ensure they don't accidentally slip into a compromising situation, such as being alone in the dark. You can find books in your local Christian bookstore that will give you wise guidance on the subject.

Some parents have bought a promise ring for their son or daughter. This ring is a symbol of his or her commitment to the Lord to remain pure until the day they are married. Remember, you don't want to simply tell them, "Stop doing it because I said so, or because the Bible says so." The Bible is full of reasons *why*. As you give your teen biblical principles to stand on, they will be more willing to stand up and do the right thing. I have seen this happen over and over again.

God bless you as you instill moral fiber in your young person and help them get a renewed sense of purity and dignity about their future intimacy with their spouse.

23

What to do if your young person was raped or involved in a date rape

This is a tragedy none of us want to be faced with or ever want our daughter to be faced with. According to national statistics, one out of every three girls will be raped some time in her life. In America, a woman is raped once every six minutes. A majority of children surveyed by a Rhode Island Rape Crisis Center thought rape was acceptable, and in New York City rape arrests of 13-year-old boys have increased 200 percent in the past two years.

It happens far more often than we would like to admit — often in the form of what is called "date rape," when a young lady is pushed beyond her comfort level. She has said no a couple of times and is with someone she knows and doesn't think will push the issue any further. But when it's all said and done, she is not really sure what happened. She never intended to let it happen. She is not really sure if she allowed it, since there was no screaming or fighting involved. She feels violated. She is embarrassed and ashamed. In most cases, she is afraid to tell anyone, especially her parents.

One young lady said,

"I lied to my parents and told them I was going to a friend's house. I went out drinking with my guy friends and then dancing. One of them got mad and beat me until I was unconscious. I had asked the other guys to take me home, but they ended up taking me somewhere else. Three of them raped me. My parents grounded me for six months and never took me to the doctor or even talked to me about it."

Listen to what other young people have said:

"I had sex with my boyfriend. They didn't know it wasn't my choice. My mother told me that I had completely ruined my life and wouldn't speak to me for a long time."

"After I had been raped, I wish my parents had not made me feel guilty for 'allowing it' to happen. I wish they had been there for love and support."

Only 20 percent of sexual assaults are by strangers. In San Diego, four of five rape victims reported that their perpetrators were acquaintances or friends. In a recent survey, 56 percent of high school girls and 76 percent of boys thought forced sex was acceptable sometimes. Fifty-one percent of boys and 41 percent of girls said that forced sex was acceptable if the boy "spent a lot of money" on the girl. Sixty-five percent of boys and 47 percent of girls said it was acceptable for a boy to rape a girl if they had dated for more than six months.[1]

SEX

You can't believe everything you hear — especially about rape. What are some of the most common myths about this crime?

Myth #1: Rape is no big deal. It's just sex.

Truth: Rape is not just sex — it's a violent crime which uses a sexual weapon. Rape can cause long-term emotional, physical, and mental damage.

Myth #2: It's not really rape if you're attacked by someone you know.

Truth: Four out of five rapists are known by the victims. Acquaintances are as capable of committing rape as anyone.

Myth #3: Date rape is not really a rape because the woman agreed to go out with the man, and therefore led them on to believe she was sexually interested.

Truth: Any forced sex is rape, whether the violator be friend, familiar face, or foe. When a woman agrees to go out with a man, she is not automatically agreeing to any sexual activity. No matter how much the man spends on the woman, or how attracted they think they are to her, to force sexual activity is to rape her.

Myth #4: The woman always has to try to physically fight the man off before it's considered rape. The charge is based on the strength of her resistance.

Truth: In many states, a man who persists when a woman verbally says "no" is considered a rapist. Many states also say a woman doesn't have to say "no"; it's rape if she doesn't specifically say "yes," if she is too intoxicated, or otherwise unable to make a sound judgment. Some organizations are pressing for new laws to charge men with rape when they psychologically coerce women into unwanted sex.

Myth #5: The perpetrator acted out of love.

Truth: Love respects, is kind, and gives. Love does not hurt another or demand to control that person.

Myth #6: Only young, pretty women are victims.

Truth: Rape happens to women, and occasionally men, of all ages, sizes, races, and appearances. Because rape is a violent crime, it is not one caused by the temptation of beauty.

Myth #7: The rapist is simply oversexed.

Truth: The rapist is an emotionally off-balanced person who uses forced sex to gain control.

Myth #8: The rapist is a child who cannot control their new sexual feelings.

Truth: No matter their age, the rapist knows what they are doing. They are acting not from sexual desire, but from misplaced anger.

Myth #9: The victims asked for it.

Truth: No one asks for something horrible to happen to her. No matter what the victim does or says, this does not give someone else the right to abuse that person.

Myth #10: Women have secret fantasies about being raped.

Truth: Men who believe this myth have a misconception about the emotional make-up of women.

Myth #11: If the woman says "no" but lets you kiss her, she means "yes" or wants you to persuade her.

Truth: No means no. Just because a woman feels attracted to a man and lets him kiss her does not mean she wants to be raped. If she's having a hard time putting her head above her hormones or emotions, this does not give the man the right to take advantage of her.

Myth #12: It's not really rape unless it's intercourse.

Truth: In most states, any kind of forced sexual activity is considered rape, including anal or oral sex and other sexual liberties.[2]

You may find yourself in a situation where your daughter has been violated in this way. What should you do?

In *Parents and Teenagers*, Janice Short gives seven practical guidelines (and I have added one of my own) for responding to the shock of your daughter's rape:

1. Believe her story.

2. React to the news with a nonjudgmental and supportive attitude.

3. Don't treat your daughter like she is damaged property.

4. Talk openly about the rape.

5. Avoid being overprotective or patronizing.

6. Accept her emotions, even if you don't understand them.

7. Seek counseling for yourself.[3]

8. Be very caring and loving towards your daughter.

Too many times a parent blames the daughter and says, "You weren't really raped. You wanted it to happen. You were being too promiscuous. You led that guy on." It is amazing how many teenagers have unsupportive parents, so they are afraid to even tell them what happened. They hide behind silent sadness and deep hurt over what happened. This tragedy is compounded by the fact that they feel they cannot talk to anyone about it.

If your daughter does come to you, reach out your arms and let her know you love her. You believe her. You are going to stand with her. She is going to struggle with feeling dirty, unworthy, and impure as a result of this. Do not let stigma come from you as a result of your attitude toward her.

Jesus said in Luke 4:18 that He came "to bind up the broken-hearted." That is, Jesus came to take the brokenhearted in His hands, love them, pick up the pieces of their heart and put them back together again. That is the role you need to play as a parent.

If she has not come to you about a situation like this, it is particularly important for you to pay attention to her attitudes and behavior regarding any and all dating experiences. First of all, as I stated in chapter 21, make sure you have prayed about your teen's dating relationships. You must have that inner peace from God.

Get well acquainted with the person your daughter is about to go out with — not just his name. Spend some time with him. Have him come over to the house a few times for dinner before allowing your daughter to go out with him. You need to be confident he has the character to treat your daughter with dignity and respect — or don't you dare let him take her out!

Once he has passed the approval process, which may take several weeks or even months, be sure to know all of their plans for the evening. Know where they will be and what time your daughter will be home. Maybe have your daughter call and check in the first few times they go out.

Be sure, either that night or the next morning, to talk about how the date went — look into her eyes, look at her demeanor, see how she carries herself. Is she really herself with you? You are watching for signs. Maybe something happened that she is ashamed of or doesn't want to tell you about. Not that you are trying to be a detective, but if a tragedy has happened, you want to be the first one to rescue her and help her pick up the pieces.

Contact the authorities. Go about this carefully so as to protect the privacy of your daughter and your family. Whether or not it seems like your daughter had an active part in luring this guy, the authorities should still be contacted. A police report should be made. That guy should be stopped before he does it to someone else.

Contact your pastor and youth pastor. Get people praying for your daughter and your family. God can use those in leadership at your church to help bind up broken hearts, put the pieces back together, and be a source of encouragement as you walk through this process of restoring wholeness to your daughter and your family.

Find a good Christian counselor, or one of the pastoral staff at your church, to talk through the painful issues of forgiveness, wholeness, and purity. There are too many parents who think, "Just get over it. Put a bandage on it. It will be okay." They would rather put it out of their mind and pretend it didn't happen. It didn't happen to you, but it did happen to your daughter, and she can't pretend it didn't.

It will take some time to really talk through some issues to bring freedom and wholeness to her. Don't get impatient with the process. Know that it takes time for complete restoration to happen. Ask God to fill you with His grace, mercy, and love, as you walk through this together and come out a stronger family.

Most importantly, let them know how much God loves them! He is not ashamed of her for what happened. He wants to comfort her, love her, and give her peace. Although it may seem like it to her, her life is not over. He has great plans for her and *good* things for her. Encourage her to seek the Lord and turn to Him in this time of trouble.

He who dwells in the shelter of the Most High will rest in the shadow of the Almighty.

Psalm 91:1

This is love: not that we loved God, but that he loved us and sent his Son as an atoning sacrifice for our sins.

1 John 4:10

God is our refuge and strength, an ever-present help in trouble.

Psalm 46:1

Brothers, I do not consider myself yet to have taken hold of it. But one thing I do: Forgetting what is behind and straining toward what is ahead, I press on toward the goal to win the prize for which God has called me heavenward in Christ Jesus.

Philippians 3:13,14

He lifted me out of the slimy pit, out of the mud and mire; he set my feet on a rock and gave me a firm place to stand. He put a new song in my mouth, a hymn of praise to our God. Many will see and fear and put their trust in the Lord.

Psalm 40:2,3

Your daughter and your family will forever remember how you respond in this time of crisis. Getting mad at yourself, the perpetrator, or at your daughter, will not resolve the issue. Responding with lots of mercy, understanding, and compassion is what you want to stick in her mind. She will think back on this and remember how her mother and father wrapped themselves around her heart and her life like a protective cocoon as she journeyed down the road to recovery.

24

What to do if your young person is contemplating suicide and how to know the signs

Far more young people contemplate suicide than one might suspect. Every 90 minutes in America, a young person kills himself. One-third of all teenagers in the United States say they have considered suicide — 15 percent have thought about it seriously and 6 percent have actually tried to kill themselves, according to a Gallup Poll.

Forty-seven percent say it is because of family problems, 22 percent say they are depressed, and 22 percent say they have problems with friends and peer pressure. Suicide is the second leading cause of death for adolescents, accidents being the first. Ironically, many accidents are suspected to be suicide-related. By the year 2000, it is projected that there will be well over 250,000 people per year who will attempt suicide. We as parents must know the telltale signs of a young person considering suicide and what to do about it.

It is interesting that most teen suicides are not among the poor and unpopular. Many of those who both attempt and commit suicide are those you would least expect — those who look like they have everything going for them and are very popular.

Signs of suicidal tendencies include:

1. Changes in eating and sleeping habits

2. Withdrawal from friends and family activities

3. Violent or rebellious behavior (i.e., running away)

4. Drug or alcohol abuse

5. Changes in hygiene

6. Persistent boredom, difficulty concentrating, decline in schoolwork

7. Frequent stomachaches, headaches, and fatigue

8. Loss of interest in pleasurable activities

9. Inability to accept praise

10. Feeling "rotten inside"

11. Giving away favorite possessions

12. Verbal hints such as, "I won't see you again"[1]

Eighty percent of suicide victims communicate their intention to someone beforehand. The problem is, most people don't take them seriously. If you see any of these tendencies in your young person, it is important to take it very seriously. Examine what is going on in their life and how you can help them get through it.

What should you do if you see some of these signs in your young person's life?

Pray! I don't mean pray a little prayer and hope things get better. I mean, pray a prayer of faith over your young person. Rebuke the spirit of death off of their life. Jesus said in John 10:10, **The thief comes only to steal and kill and destroy.** If your young person is thinking in any way that life is not worth living and that they should end it, the enemy of their souls is trying to deceive them. The devil is the one who wants your teen to die before their appointed time.

Pray, "In Jesus' name, Satan, you cannot have my young person. I rebuke you in the name of Jesus. You stay away. They will live and not die. They will fulfill God's plan for their life." Pray a prayer of faith like that over them and deal with the core root problem.

These aren't just words you can say and then expect the enemy to go running away with his tail between his legs. You have to pray this until you know deep within your heart you have truly taken authority over every evil one. He gave authority to His disciples to drive out evil spirits and He has given that authority to us. (See Matthew 10:1 and Luke 10:19.)

Speak scriptures over your teen and over your home. (See the end of this chapter for suggested Bible verses.) Go into their bedroom while they are at school or work and lay hands on and pray over their bed, their clothes, and anoint with oil their door-post and bedroom walls. Rebuke the enemy from their room

CRISIS SITUATIONS

and invite the Holy Spirit in. Place a hedge of divine protection around their physical being, actively taking authority.

If your young person has attempted, seriously contemplated, or talked about committing suicide, do not take this lightly. They are crying out for help! Get them into professional care right away for an evaluation. I would suggest a program like Rapha, which is a Christian counseling ministry.

Really listen to your young person. Never underestimate the seriousness of a threat or suggested harm to themselves. Listen carefully to their emotions and plans. They may have planned a very specific way to end their life. If so, it is a much more serious situation than you may have first thought.

Empathize with them. Don't just patronize, put down, or shrug off their feelings of loneliness, emptiness, and worthlessness. Empathizing means reflecting what they are saying with *your* own words, trying with all your heart to put yourself in their shoes. "I can understand how you feel." "You must be feeling really bad."

Many times if you dismiss their feelings with, "You shouldn't feel like that, you should feel like this," your teen will feel like you are not really listening to them, not really connected, and not really caring about them. As you empathize, reinforce the fact that you recognize what they are feeling.

Just being there as a compassionate friend/parent can often diffuse a young person's sense of being all alone in their pain. If they can see in your eyes and in your heart that you are right there with them every step of the way, they will not feel so isolated and alone. They won't feel like they have to deal with the situation all by themselves.

Here are some specific things you can do, based on the work of Jay Adams, Marianne Dougworth, and Bill Blackburn:

1. Work on your relationship with them as it relates to different issues. Don't just be interested in talking to them about their thoughts of suicide, but talk to them about their life, their heart, their direction and goals, their passion, and their failures and successes. The best prevention for suicide is a healthy, strong relationship with parents and with other people. You will never really "arrive" in a relationship — it must be something you are continually working on.

2. Build self-worth. It is important to help your teen build their self-worth, but not in a patronizing way. Don't just say, "Well, you're good at this, and you're good at that," every time they feel bad about themselves. Begin building their self-worth when you are not in a counseling session or in a deep conversation about suicide. When they say something witty, identify it. When they say something intelligent, comment on it. When they do something good, compliment them. You are looking for any reason to give them hope, taking little baby steps along the way.

3. Instill hope in them. Adams says, "Suicidal persons need hope. They are preeminently persons with no hope." Give them hope that things will get better, hope in their heart that God created them for a specific purpose. Build their hope and begin to build their faith. Teach your young person where suicidal thoughts come from. The enemy wants to destroy their life and destroy their soul, but God wants to give them abundant life. (See John 10:10.) God wants to bless them and all the hope and faith for an incredible life is found in Him alone. The people who know their God shall

be strong and do exploits. (See Daniel 11:32 KJV.) I can do all things through Christ who strengthens me. (See Philippians 4:13.) As you share scriptures with them, it will build faith and hope in their heart that they can get over this cesspool of depression.

4. Teach coping skills. With all the pressures, temptations, frustrations, and confusion your young person faces, teach them positive steps they can take when they face those crises; they do not have to feel hopeless or that they will never get over it. Impart to them principles on how to live life so, when they feel they're at the end of their rope, when they get an F on a test, or when they don't do well in sports, they don't feel like throwing in the towel. You cannot expect to just sit down with them one time and tell them some neat things to do that you read in a book. Coping skills must be reinforced on a regular basis. Constantly impart to them, "This is how you deal with life. This is how you deal with tough situations." Role play and talk through situations so that when they find themselves in one of those situations, they have the answers already prepared. This is called parenting. It's more than putting food in their stomach and a roof over their head — it's teaching them how to deal with life.

5. Develop a plan of action. If they start considering suicide, what will you do? Develop a plan of action to deal with some of the most bothersome circumstances that make them feel hopeless. Help *them* develop a plan — how will they get out of this? How will they improve their situation? Don't just say, "Oh, you'll get over it," but help them find a way out by developing a plan of action. If a plan of action isn't obvious, research until you come up with one. Maybe

a good plan would be for them to throw some of their energy into something new, fun, and interesting, such as horseback riding, a sport, or a project the two of you can work on together.

Finally, draw your teen into a personal commitment to prevent a suicide attempt. If they start feeling depressed or thinking about suicide, they agree to contact you. They agree not to quit trying to contact you until they get through to you. Keep a pager or a cell phone with you and agree to call them back at the first available moment. Commit to staying with them once they contact you until the crisis has passed. It requires commitment on both parts — from you and your young person — to really deal with this.

Make yourself 100 percent available — if that means interrupting a meeting or getting off an important phone call, do it! No situation is more important than supporting your son or daughter in an intense time like this. Constantly reaffirm this commitment as you get together and talk.

Please realize that just because you have a plan like this, it is not the ultimate plan. The ultimate plan is to instill hope, faith, and vision for their future. Constantly let your young person know that God has a great plan for their life and you are praying for them. Speak words of faith over them.

Get them more concerned about the future and about reaching out to *others* and helping them. That will help draw them out of the depression. Pour your energy into helping them develop a vision for their future — a plan of faith and optimism. Ask God to birth a dream in your teen's heart of what He wants to do with their life. If they are consumed with God's plan for their life and His hope for their future, they will be drawn further away from suicide and will begin to love and enjoy life.

Begin praying these scripture verses over your teen:

> **No evil will befall you, nor will any plague come near your tent. For He will give His angels charge concerning you, to guard you in all your ways.**
>
> **Psalm 91:10,11** NASB

> **For He delivered us from the domain of darkness, and transferred us to the kingdom of His beloved Son.**
>
> **Colossians 1:13** NASB

> **No weapon that is formed against you shall prosper.**
>
> **Isaiah 54:17** NASB

> **But you are a chosen people, a royal priesthood, a holy nation, a people belonging to God, that you may declare the praises of him who called you out of darkness into his wonderful light.**
>
> **1 Peter 2:9**

> **But as for me and my household, we will serve the Lord.**
>
> **Joshua 24:15**

If you find yourself facing this situation, you also need strength and encouragement for yourself that only the Word of God can offer. Rely on the Holy Spirit to comfort and guide you in all your ways.

God is our refuge and strength, an ever-present help in trouble.

Psalm 46:1

The joy of the Lord is your strength.

Nehemiah 8:10

But thanks be to God! He gives us the victory through our Lord Jesus Christ.

1 Corinthians 15:57

For our struggle is not against flesh and blood, but against the rulers, against the authorities, against the powers of this dark world and against the spiritual forces of evil in the heavenly realms.

Ephesians 6:12

I will give you the keys of the kingdom of heaven; whatever you bind on earth will be bound in heaven, and whatever you loose on earth will be loosed in heaven.

Matthew 16:19

When I am afraid, I will trust in you.

Psalm 56:3

CRISIS SITUATIONS

We demolish arguments and every pretension that sets itself up against the knowledge of God, and we take captive every thought to make it obedient to Christ.

2 Corinthians 10:5

Yet this I call to mind and therefore I have hope: Because of the Lord's great love we are not consumed, for his compassions never fail. They are new every morning; great is your faithfulness.

Lamentations 3:21-23

"For I know the plans I have for you," declares the Lord, "plans to prosper you and not to harm you, plans to give you hope and a future."

Jeremiah 29:11

God has wonderful plans for your teen. He has a purpose for their life. Stand on the promises of His Word and you will have the victory.

25

What to do when your teen is in trouble with the law

The phone rings. You search for the clock... 1:30 A.M.?! Who could possibly be calling at such an hour? Scrambling to find the phone, various scenarios rush through your mind — a car accident, a sudden illness, death of a loved one — while the names of your family members run through your head.

You finally grab the phone and manage to grunt out a weak hello. An official sounding voice on the other end asks, "Are you the parents of _____?" You quickly respond, "Yes, I am."

In the ensuing few moments you discover your teen has broken the law and is in jail for the night. Terror grips your soul! You are shocked with horror and disbelief! This stuff happens to other people's kids, not yours. Surely there has been a mistake. They must have the wrong parents, the wrong child, and the wrong number. But it is not the wrong number.

Your teen is incarcerated and you have to be able to think clearly. How should you respond? Who should you call? Should you try to bail them out or let them sit in the jail cell for one night? What should you do?

Here are several principles to use in responding to this situation.

Be compassionate. No matter how brokenhearted, mad, hurt, or angry you might be, it is important you respond with compassion. Even though you don't like what they have done, your young person must know you accept them and still love them.

Look at the story of the prodigal son in Luke 15:11-32. The son took his inheritance, went away, spent it all on prostitutes and parties, and became a disgrace to his family. Although his father was very wealthy, the son ended up in another country working as a slave and serving pigs. When he realized he had done wrong, he came running back to his father.

It's important to note what the father did. Even though he had been deeply hurt and his dreams and goals for his son had been shattered, as soon as he saw his son returning, he ran to him, threw his arms around him, and welcomed him home.

It is important for you to respond with the same kind of attitude. No matter what your child has done, they are still your son or daughter. Your love and acceptance should be unconditional — just as God's love is for us. (See John 13:34.)

At the same time, you want them to realize the gravity of the situation. You don't want them to think, "No big deal. It's really not that bad of a thing because they still love me." Let them know you don't approve of their actions. They have hurt their parents and maybe other family members. But also let them know you love them and are committed to their success.

I heard a story of a well-known pastor whose son had been drifting further and further away from his family and from the Lord. After the son made a huge mistake and landed in jail, the father went to visit him. Having a distant and cold relationship, the son wasn't sure how his father would respond. But the father looked into his son's eyes and said, "How can I help you?"

Those words tore down the wall standing between father and son. The son began to weep uncontrollably in his father's arms. Instead of condemning him or telling him he was no good, the father emphasized the fact that he was still his son and he still loved him. Their relationship was restored and the son is no longer in jail or in trouble with the law.

Accept responsibility. "I know my child didn't really *mean* to do something wrong or illegal." Whether it was driving under the influence, armed robbery, petty theft, or vandalism, you are tempted to think, "They just got caught with the wrong crowd."

This rationale is dangerous, because it takes the responsibility off the young person. In essence, you believe it's not really their fault, because they are a good kid. They were just with the wrong people at the wrong time. If it is not their responsibility, you can rationalize that they didn't do anything wrong. Because of embarrassment and not wanting to admit that your kid could have done something wrong, you dismiss the fact that it really is at least partially their responsibility.

Most parents think this is just a one-time thing. It's a fluke — an accident. You'll get them out of jail, off the hook, and everything will be fine — no problem. You must understand, it may be the first time in jail, but it certainly isn't the first step to getting into that situation.

CRISIS SITUATIONS

In previous chapters, I discussed the importance of your young person's friends. Trouble with the law is another pitfall of hanging out with the wrong crowd. Drinking, smoking, ditching school, staying out late, and other incremental steps often lead to criminal activity. Most parents do not want to believe their kids would do any of those things. Then, when something more serious happens, they minimize it as one little thing, when in reality, it is the culmination of a series of bad decisions.

Maybe you don't know your child as well as you thought you did. If you dismiss this offense as an isolated incident, you're not seeing the picture for what it really is and you will not solve the problem. You may get them out of jail, but the problem still remains.

What brought them to the point of stepping too close to the edge, doing something really stupid, and getting thrown in jail? What decisions could have been made differently for a better outcome? Instead of just getting them out of jail and off the hook, see how you and your teen can keep this from happening again.

You are to influence and mold them. Make sure they are not hanging around friends that could get them into trouble. Don't allow them to stay out late or go to places that could result in a huge downfall. And remember, *you* are their example. Your own actions and standards speak louder than any lecture can.

Instead of trying to deny that your teen is really like this, get to know them. Make your teen your first priority. Develop a relationship with them. Allow them to provide you with insight as to why they want to do the things they do. They aren't a bad person — they simply need direction and guidance.

Accept the consequences. Our first reaction is to get them out of trouble. We don't want them to embarrass us. We don't want them to mess up their life. We don't want them to have a criminal record. We can't stand the thought of having them fully pay the price and suffer the consequences. Other people can pay for what they did, but not our son or daughter!

Be careful if you are thinking like this. It may very well damage your young person more than it will help them. They have committed a serious infraction or they wouldn't be in jail. If you bail them out now, you might be bailing them out the rest of their life.

It is important they accept responsibility and pay the price for what they have done. This doesn't mean just a mild slap on the wrist. Allowing them to face the consequences the first time will most likely deter them from further wrongdoing. Dr. James Dobson calls this *tough love.*

Some might say, "But I thought I was to love them. Wouldn't loving them mean getting them off the hook?" Not necessarily — there's a difference between having grace and forgiveness towards a person and bailing them out of trouble time and again.

In our society, if someone robs a bank and asks the Lord to forgive them He does, but they still have to face the consequences. His grace and forgiveness is there for us, but there are still consequences. God wants us to be responsible people.

I was involved with a family whose teenage son had been part of an armed robbery. During the robbery, the store tenant was killed. These Christian parents didn't know what to do. Their options were to have their son turn himself in, or to have him flee the country, since he hadn't been caught.

If he turned himself in, they knew the law would take its full course. If he fled the country, he would be running the rest of his life. He decided to turn himself in. The parents got the best attorney they could find and went to court.

Through it all, this young man really turned his life over to the Lord. He did go to jail, but he stayed close to the Lord throughout his jail time. He experienced time in jail as a consequence to his crime, but he also experienced God's compassion and grace. Now, out of jail and in full-time ministry, this situation has been turned around and has brought glory and honor to God. (See Romans 8:28.)

If it had been possible, these parents would have tried to get him completely off the hook so he wouldn't have to serve jail time. But it wasn't possible, and it was definitely not wise.

In some cases, an attorney can get their young person off on a lesser charge, or completely prevent them from serving time or probation, yet the teenager hasn't learned anything. Having to face tough consequences serves as a huge reminder and milestone for the rest of their life that this is something they do not want to repeat!

If you find yourself rescuing your teenager from the hole they've dug for themselves, you will find yourself doing it again and again and again. If they never learn by having to pay the price for their actions, they will live their life with the mindset that, no matter what they do, they will *never* have to suffer the consequences.

Involve your pastor. Ask your pastor to visit your son or daughter. Ask for his counsel on what went wrong and search the Scriptures on what to do next. You don't want to go through this situation alone. You need a few close Christian friends and the leaders of the church praying for your family and encouraging you. Don't fight this battle all alone.

Don't be so full of pride that you think you can handle it by yourself. Yes, it is embarrassing, but people are going to find out anyway. You might as well tell those who love you so they can stand with you and pray for you.

Incorporate preventive measures. If your child has not broken the law, there are some preventive measures you can take. The first one is *discipline*. We need to teach our children about discipline when they are young. This is more than spankings — it is learning to live a disciplined life.

Does your young person know what your standards are? Teach them to abide faithfully by the rules you have set at home as well as the rules society sets up as our governing laws. If they learn to honor authorities, leaders, rules, regulations, and laws, their life will be blessed.

Teach them the difference between right and wrong. Set disciplinary measures and be prepared to follow through with them. Even as teenagers in your home, they need to know they will have to pay a price if they go beyond what you permit. That price may be no television, no social activities, or no telephone privileges. If you teach them there are consequences for their actions, beginning in their childhood and all the way through their teen years, they will understand that they have to suffer those consequences.

CRISIS SITUATIONS

Teens need to learn to live their lives within the parameters, rules, and laws set for them. We contradict ourselves and undermine our parenting when we rescue them all the time. They may get in trouble at school. They may yell at their teacher or the principal. They may fall in with the wrong crowd and succumb to peer pressure. They may even get suspended from school. But rescuing them from these situations will teach them that they never have to pay the price. Mom and Dad will always be there to divert the blame. What we consider to be *protecting* them is actually preventing them from becoming productive and responsible members of society.

Teach them to *respect* and *obey* laws and authority figures by your example. Do you bad-mouth the teacher, the coach, the instructor, or the principal? Do you speak ill of them behind their backs? Do you observe the governing laws set for you? If your child's teacher carries out disciplinary measures, are you quick to come to the defense of your child, believing your child could do absolutely nothing wrong? If so, this is damaging your child!

Everyone must submit himself to the governing authorities, for there is no authority except that which God has established. The authorities that exist have been established by God. Consequently, he who rebels against the authority is rebelling against what God has instituted, and those who do so will bring judgment on themselves. Therefore, it is necessary to submit to the authorities, not only because of possible punishment but also because of conscience.

Romans 13:1,2,5

CHAPTER TWENTY-FIVE . . . **WHAT TO DO WHEN YOUR TEEN IS IN TROUBLE WITH THE LAW**

Laws, rules, and regulations are set up by God to establish order. We stay out of trouble because we know there will be a price to pay, but also because disobedience is considered rebellion against God. Teach your teen that submitting to authority is not only the right and honorable thing to do, it is the godly thing to do.

What happens when the court proceedings are over, when they are out of jail, or when their probation time is up? Is it really over? Hopefully this incident has served as a wake-up call.

Are you still showing that unconditional love? This time can be the beginning of a brand-new journey for you and your teen. You should be excited to get to know them — to find out what makes them tick! Spend time with them, doing fun things. Listen to them and discover what is in their heart. Look for opportunities to teach them the principles that will keep them close to God and away from further legal trouble. Help them find their place — right in the middle of God's will — so they can begin experiencing His richest blessings on their life.

26

What to do if your young person is obsessed with wild clothes, hair, and body piercings

There you are, thinking you are raising a relatively normal child. You have done beautifully through their childhood years. Now in their early teen years it looks like everything is going well, but you've begun to notice some subtle changes in the way they dress. They don't like their normal clothes anymore. They want to wear weird styles with drab, dark colors. You notice their hair begins to look increasingly offbeat and not what most people would think normal.

Your daughter is beginning to create strange effects with her makeup. You notice unusual jewelry around her neck, ankles, fingers, and wrists. She has more than one hole pierced in her ear. Your son comes home with an earring in his ear — or more than one earring. Some young people will actually come home with multiple piercings in their ears, their nose, their tongue, their eyebrows, and their navel. Others will just talk about it as a joke, just to see how mom and dad will respond.

You are wondering how far to let this go. Is it just a phase your teen is going through? Is it something they will get over? Is it just a fad like blue jeans and T-shirts were in the '50s? Or is this something you should be concerned about?

It is particularly striking and shocking if your young person makes these outward physical changes overnight. When you see them with all the piercings and weird clothing styles, you wonder if they are still your child. You grab them and say, "Who are you?! What have you done with my teenager?!?!"

What is a parent to do? Realize this is still your child, although their hair, earrings, and clothes might look extremely bizarre. If your teen is already dressing like this or is beginning to get into it, it is imperative you put the emphasis on your relationship with them and how much you care about them.

Be cautious about tearing them down because of what they look like, what they are wearing, or what jewelry they have on. Although you may strongly, vehemently disagree with it (as I do), if your approval of them is based on how they look, they will think your love is conditional.

Right now, more than ever, you must engage them in conversations that draw their heart back towards you. Don't just talk about their body piercings and hair all the time. Talk to them as a person — what they are thinking, what they are feeling, what they are going through. Get to know them all over again.

If this has happened overnight, it has probably struck you with, "I thought I knew my child. How could they possibly have done this?!" You probably did not know them as well as you thought you did. It's time to get reacquainted with your young person.

Should you be concerned about this kind of behavior? Absolutely, yes! Do not put it off as another phase your young person is going through. The mainstream of teenagers today in the '90s is not behaving this way. There is definitely an element participating in these kinds of activities, but it is not the mainstream, so you do need to be concerned.

Look into the eyes and the heart of your young person to see what's going on inside. The problem is not what they did with their hair or body. The problem is the attitude that led them to do it — the need for peer acceptance and the need to "make a statement" that pressured them to feel they had to do it. What kind of statement are they making? Who influenced them to think that by doing this they would be making that statement? From a band? From a friend? Who are these friends?

> **Do not conform any longer to the pattern of this world, but be transformed by the renewing of your mind.**
>
> **Romans 12:2**

When God looks at your teen, He does not look at all this stuff on the outside, but He definitely looks at what is going on inside. What makes them feel like they have to dress in an outlandish way in order to communicate a point? Many will say they are trying to be an individual — it is who they are. That is definitely questionable. Is that really who they are?

Of course, in their own minds they are saying that is who they are because they are hearing their friends say, "This is who we are. We're making a statement." So they reason, "This is who I want to be. I want to make the same statement."

CRISIS SITUATIONS

So you're still asking, "Well, why is that so bad?" If the attitude your teen is reflecting is self-destructive, one of depression, or rebellious against society, or one that says, "I don't care what you think, I'm going to do my own thing," then obviously there is a real issue and a real problem.

Why do young people do this? They are identifying with some group — either a music group, a group of friends at school, at a hangout, on a ball team, or even in a youth group. Somehow it was put into their mind that if they changed their appearance like this, there would be acceptance by a particular group of people they regard as significant and want to impress or hang out with. They want to do whatever it takes to gain that acceptance.

Please understand, your teen will not see it like this. They think they are doing it to be their own individual. Your job is not to convince your teen that you know better and they are really doing it to be accepted, because they will probably never admit to that. You need to discover why they have the need to feel accepted by that particular crew.

Your job is to help your young person make sure they are surrounding themselves with the right kind of peers and not just whoever happens to be around. That is why it is so extremely important that you do not just live under the same roof and eat at the same table without really knowing what is going on in their life. You have to help shape and influence the environment your young person grows up in, which is largely their peers and friends at school and church.

Somehow your teen has woven themselves into this group of people who are now very significant to them. It is important, then, that you do not just pass off their friends as stupid kids. "Why do they dress like that??!!" The more you think and talk that way, the more it will push your teen to identify with those kids and think you are just an old parent who doesn't understand.

It is important for you to know these kids who are your teen's friends to show that you are not dismissing them without reason or without giving them a chance. At the same time, it is absolutely imperative that you help your young person find the right kind of friends you want them to be around — those destined for success, who love God with all their hearts, and who are wholesome in every area of their lives.

Search out these young people and find ways to endear your teen to them. One way might be to meet with a great youth pastor in town. Talk with him about your young person. Ask him what their youth group might have to offer and what they could do to reach out and pull your young person in as a friend and a companion.

If your young person is a Christian and has been raised in church, they might be thinking, "I just want to reach out to other young people who are dressed like this." I caution you to be careful of that. Although it sounds legitimate on the surface, there is still great cause for concern.

Maybe your young person has a heart to minister to kids who are dressing and acting like this, so they start dressing like this and doing their hair like them. They begin to talk to them, get to know them, and do all the right things to develop a relationship so they can evangelize them. But then they start listening to them so much, they begin to defend them.

"You know what? These kids really have been misunderstood. There really are a lot of hypocrites out there. The church really doesn't understand them. I can't believe the church doesn't accept them. They went to this one church and they got so mistreated." They take on the offenses of these young people. Pretty soon they are more committed to and drawn to the people they are trying to reach out to than they are with their Christian friends.

How far do we need to go to relate and reach out in order to effectively minister? Jesus did hang out with prostitutes. He hung out in bars. But He did not become like them. He didn't dress like them. He didn't even spend most of His time with them. He spent most of His time with His disciples. So your teen's core peer group and the people they are best friends with and have the most camaraderie with should be the people who love God with all their heart — wholesome, strong individuals.

When reaching out and ministering to people who are dressed like this, it should be perceived as a ministry venture, not something they are going out on their own to do — and hope they survive spiritually. Do not play this down. It is so important they do not identify more with the group they are trying to reach out to than with a group that is loving God, has wholesome values, and a wholesome way of representing the Christian life.

What they want to do is noble, but there have been too many tragic stories of young people who have fallen away from God, because in seeking to identify, they got sucked into a peer group and pulled away from God.

WHAT TO DO IF YOUR YOUNG PERSON IS OBSESSED WITH WILD CLOTHES, HAIR, AND BODY PIERCINGS

If your teen is dressing and acting like this, should you immediately say, "Stop it right now!"? It depends on where they are. If they are just barely starting to change, you know their heart is still with you, and they still love God with all their heart, then yes, stop it right away — even if they don't understand.

If their heart is already gone and you say, "No more!" you could push them over the edge to say, "I'm going to do what I want to do anyway!" You have to be much more careful and diplomatic at how you woo their heart back towards you. You can enforce a rule at home, but as soon as they walk out the door, if their identity is still wrapped up with that group, your teen will put all the jewelry and earrings back on, and you have still lost them.

Your teen may not do it around you, but they will do it out of your sight; so you have lost the real battle. Some parents might say, "Well, as long as they don't do it around me, it's okay." No, it is not okay! That is not what you want. You want your young person's heart. You want their relationship. If they are already beyond that, you must be honest with yourself and realize you will have to be more tactful.

Begin to pull them in, get to know their friends, and diplomatically work through a strategy to get them involved with other wholesome young people. They will go through the motions — combing their hair right and wearing the right clothes in front of you if they must. But if you have their *hair* and not their *heart*, you don't really have them. Talk it over with your spouse and with your pastor. See what the best way to approach the issue would be.

CRISIS SITUATIONS

If your young person has not started this, begin to talk about it. Make sure they understand that you won't allow it in your home. If they talk about it in any way, jokingly or alluding to doing it, that's a sign for you to start emphasizing your relationship with them.

Spend time with them and talk with them, so their heart is immediately drawn back to you. Don't even give their heart a chance to escape or to be drawn towards others who have succumbed to these kinds of actions and attitudes of rebellion.

Endnotes

Chapter 1

[1] Jay Kesler, *Ten Mistakes Parents Make With Teenagers* (Wolgemuth & Hyatt Publishers, 1988).

Chapter 2

[1] Kathleen McCoy, Ph.D., "Teen Rebellion: What's Normal, What's Not."

[2] James Dobson, *Parenting Isn't for Cowards* (Dallas, TX: Word Books, 1996) p. 145.

[3] Josh McDowell, *Josh McDowell's Handbook on Counseling Youth* (Dallas, TX: Word Books, 1996) pp. 235-236.

Chapter 3

[1] *USA Today*, March 26, 1996.

[2] George Barna, *Generation Next* (Ventura, CA: Regal Books, 1997) p. 100.

[3] Ibid., p. 101.

Chapter 4

[1] *GROUP Magazine,* March 1994, p. 29.

Chapter 6

[1] James Dobson, *Parenting Isn't for Cowards* (Dallas, TX: Word Books, 1996) pp. 164-165.

[2] Jay Kesler with Ronald A. Beers, eds., *Parents and Teenagers* (Colorado Springs, CO: Victor Books, 1984) p. 118.

[3] Mike Yorkey, ed., *The Christian Family Answer Book* (Colorado Springs, CO: Chariot Books, 1996) pp. 42-44.

Chapter 7

1 *Newsweek,* June 17, 1996.

2 *Reader's Digest,* February 1997, p. 65.

3 Mike Yorkey, ed., *The Christian Family Answer Book* (Colorado Springs, CO: Chariot Books, 1996) p. 42.

4 William Beausay II, *Boys! Shaping Ordinary Boys into Extraordinary Men* (Nashville, TN: Thomas Nelson, 1994).

Chapter 8

1 *Smart Money,* September 1995.

2 *Josh McDowell's Handbook on Counseling Youth* (Dallas, TX: Word Books, 1996) pp. 197-206.

3 David R. Miller, *Counseling Families After Divorce* (Dallas, TX: Word Books, 1994) p. 220.

4 *USA Today,* January 4, 1996.

Chapter 9

1 *Parade Magazine,* November 10, 1996.

2 George H. Gallup International Institute survey.

3 *USA Today* poll of 703 high school student leaders.

4 *Group Magazine,* February 1996.

Chapter 10

1 *USA Today* poll of 703 high school student leaders.

2 Alexander W. Astin, Kenneth C. Green, William S. Korn and Marilynn Schalit, *The American Freshman: National Norms for Fall 1987* (Los Angeles, CA: Higher Education Research Institute, Graduate School of Education, University of California, December 1987) pp. 50,58.

3 Ibid., p. 58.

4 Mike Yorkey, ed., *The Christian Family Answer Book* (Colorado Springs, CO: Chariot Books, 1996) p. 185.

Chapter 11

1 Quentin J. Schultze, *Winning Your Kids Back From the Media* (Downers Grove, IL: Intervarsity Press, 1994) pp. 144-145.

2 James Dobson and Gary Bauer, *Children at Risk* (Dallas, TX: Word Books, 1994) p. 65.

3 Ibid., p. 213.

Chapter 13

1   *1987 Nielsen Report on Television,* Nielsen Media Research, 1987, pp. 6-9.

2   "What Our Kids Think," *USA Today,* May 26, 1987, p. 6D.

3   *The Brown University Child and Adolescent Behavior Letter,* May 1995.

4   *GROUP Magazine,* February 1987, p. 14.

5   Quentin J. Schultze, *Winning Your Kids Back From the Media* (Downers Grove, IL: Intervarsity Press, 1994) p. 122.

6   *The Columbia,* South Carolina State, February 7, 1996.

7   George Barna, *Generation Next* (Ventura, CA: Regal Books, 1997).

8   James Dobson and Gary Bauer, *Children at Risk* (Dallas, TX: Word Books, 1994) p. 207.

9   *The Denver Post,* August 22, 1995.

10 *The Brown University Child and Adolescent Behavior Letter,* May 1995.

Chapter 14

1   *GROUP Magazine,* September/October 1996.

2   George Barna, *Generation Next* (Ventura, CA: Regal Books, 1997) p. 80.

3   *The State Newspaper,* Spring 1996.

4   Jay Kesler with Ronald A. Beers, eds., *Parents and Teenagers* (Colorado Springs, CO: Victor Books, 1984) p. 367.

5   Ibid., p. 371.

6   Ibid., p. 367.

Chapter 15

1   Gallup Survey, 1991.

2   Barna Research Group, March 18, 1996.

Chapter 17

1   *New York Times,* December 13, 1994.

2   *Entertainment Today,* March 28, 1996.

3   *Josh McDowell's Handbook on Counseling Youth* (Dallas, TX: Word Books, 1996) p. 401.

4   *USA Today,* October 22, 1996.

[5] *Josh McDowell's Handbook on Counseling Youth* (Dallas, TX: Word Books, 1996) pp. 401-402.

[6] *GROUP Magazine,* September/October 1996, p. 16.

Chapter 18

[1] Jay Kesler with Ronald A. Beers, eds., *Parents and Teenagers* (Colorado Springs, CO: Victor Books, 1984) p. 501.

[2] *The Columbia,* South Carolina State, October 18, 1995.

Chapter 19

[1] *Who's Who Among American High School Students, 1996.*

[2] Associated Press News Service, January 7, 1997.

Chapter 20

[1] Eugene C. Roehlkepartain, ed., *The Youth Ministry Resource Book* (Loveland, CO: Group Books, 1988) p. 37.

[2] Jay Kesler with Ronald A. Beers, eds., *Parents and Teenagers* (Colorado Springs, CO: Victor Books, 1984) p. 359.

[3] Jay Kesler with Ronald A. Beers, eds., *Parents and Teenagers* (Colorado Springs, CO: Victor Books, 1984).

Chapter 22

[1] *San Diego Union-Tribune/USA Today,* June 25, 1996.

[2] *Josh McDowell's Handbook on Counseling Youth* (Dallas, TX: Word Books, 1996).

[3] *GROUP Magazine,* November/December 1996.

[4] Mike Yorkey, ed., *The Christian Family Answer Book* (Colorado Springs, CO: Chariot Books, 1996) pp. 237-238.

[5] *San Diego Union-Tribune/USA TODAY,* June 25, 1996; Chicago Tribune, July 9, 1996.

Chapter 23

[1] *San Diego Union-Tribune,* September 1995.

[2] Jeanette D. Gardner, "Dispelling the Myths."

[3] Jay Kesler with Ronald A. Beers, eds., *Parents and Teenagers* (Colorado Springs, CO: Victor Books, 1984), pp. 510-511.

Ron Luce—*Profile*

President and CEO of **Teen Mania Ministries,** a national youth missions organization, based in Garden Valley, Texas. The following four areas envelope the purpose and mission of Teen Mania:

- **Missions:** Last year, 3,200 teenagers were sent out to 30 different countries. This year, Teen Mania is preparing to take 10,000 teenagers to 50 different countries.

- **ATF:** Ron hosts national youth conventions across North America called *"Acquire The Fire"*. Thousands of teens gather each weekend for a contemporary presentation of radical Christian living including mammoth video walls, a live worship band, comic sketches, and pyrotechnics. Over 147,000 teens attended last year in 27 cities. 175,000 will be attending this year in 25 cities.

- **Dome Event:** This year Ron will host Teen Mania's first dome event to be held in Pontiac, Michigan on April 23 & 24, 1999. 80,000 are expected in attendance and it will be a millennium gathering that will serve as a battle cry for this generation. "Fathers of the faith" all over the nation are standing with us at this event, as a statement that they believe in this young generation.

- **Internship/Campus:** Our Honor Academy Program disciples and develops high school graduates and college students for an entire year producing some of the finest delegates for the workplace. There are currently 519 young people enrolled in the Honor Academy and we are expecting a total class of 730 Honor Academy participants in August. Our campus consists of 464 acres and construction has been progressing quickly, developing Teen Mania into a world class facility.

Raised in a broken home and after several years of drug and alcohol abuse, Ron ran away at the age of 15 before finding Jesus at age 16.

Bachelor of Arts in psychology and theology from Oral Roberts University.

Master of Arts in counseling and psychology from the University of Tulsa.

Hosts a weekly television program called *Acquire the Fire* for teenagers, shown on Trinity Broadcasting Network.

Authored *Inspire the Fire*, a book for parents of teenagers.

Authored *56 Days Ablaze,* a devotional for teens.

Authored *Quit Playing with Fire,* a book for teenagers on how to deal with difficult issues and for parents to know how to work with their teenagers on these issues.

Authored *10 Challenges of a World Changer,* a devotional study guide, guiding readers through ten specific challenges that the teenager will commit to meet if they are to answer that call.

Authored *Mark of a World Changer,* a devotional study guide, guiding readers to make their mark on the world by building their life with character, not hype, and by utilizing the ten challenges studied in the previous devotional study guide to build that character in themselves.

Co-authored with Carman *R.I.O.T. Manual,* a book for teenagers on how to start a R.I.O.T. — Righteous Invasion Of Truth — in their own town.

Consulting Editor for the *Promise Bible for Students,* a Bible that touches base with many issues teens face today, encouraging and challenging them with words that speak their language. (CEV)

Authored *Mature Christians Are Boring People... And Other Myths About Maturing in Christ,* a devotional book for teens that identifies wrong assumptions about maturity in Christ and how to combat negative peer pressure.

Authored *Rescue Manual for Parents,* a book for parents on how to deal with pressing teen issues.

Authored *Spiritual Shock Treatment,* his latest devotional for teens.

Worship leader for five Teen Mania worship albums the latest being *Worship Shock Treatment for the Soul.*

Guest appearances on Dr. James Dobson's "Focus on the Family" radio broadcast.

Traveled to more than 50 countries, taking the Gospel to the world.

Guest host on the 700 Club and appeared several times as a guest on Trinity Broadcasting Network.

Ron and his wife Katie have three children; Hannah, Charity, and Cameron.

To contact Ron Luce or Teen Mania Ministries please write:

P. O. Box 2000
Garden Valley, Texas 75771-2000

Books by Ron Luce

Spiritual Shock Treatment —
Get Real With Jesus (Teen Devotional)

Rescue Manual for Parents

Mature Christians Are Boring People... And
Other Myths About Maturity in Christ

R.I.O.T. Manual
(co-authored with Carman)

Inspire the Fire

56 Days Ablaze

Quit Playing with Fire

10 Challenges of a WorldChanger

Mark of a WorldChanger